IMAGES
of America

GREENE COUNTY

On October 24, 1979, a catastrophic explosion and fire destroyed much of the Greene County court complex in Stanardsville and severely damaged the Greene County Courthouse. Fifteen people were injured. While firefighters labored to put out the blaze, a chain of volunteers formed a bucket brigade in 90-degree heat to rescue thousands of pages of records from the basement of the clerk's office, passing the papers through a window to those waiting outside. Archivists in Richmond later began the enormous job of restoration. The courthouse was rebuilt, although the bell in the cupola was never recovered. (Julie Dickey.)

ON THE COVER: This photograph shows pupils and teachers at Kinderhook School, which is visible in the background—one of the many small schoolhouses tucked into a hollow close to the mountains. Linwood Mitchell taught at the McMullen School in the same area. He was also a photographer. At the end of the school year, he would take a group photograph, selling copies for 25¢, and he most likely took this picture too. It looks like an early spring scene, but, as someone wrote on the wall of the Forest Hill Academy, another Greene County school: "School gets out first week of April." All hands were necessary when planting season came around. (Bobby Rhodes.)

IMAGES
of America

GREENE COUNTY

Greene County Historical Society

ARCADIA
PUBLISHING

Published by Arcadia Publishing
Charleston, South Carolina

Library of Congress Control Number: 2012941841

For all general information, please contact Arcadia Publishing:
Telephone 843-853-2070
Fax 843-853-0044
E-mail sales@arcadiapublishing.com
For customer service and orders:
Toll-Free 1-888-313-2665

Visit us on the Internet at www.arcadiapublishing.com

This book is dedicated to all those who love this very
special place and care enough to preserve its history.

CONTENTS

ACKNOWLEDGMENTS

Writing this book has taken me on an extraordinary journey through Greene County's past, a journey on which I have met with truly heartwarming assistance and encouragement from all whose help I sought.

In early 1979, the Honorable John N. Dalton, governor of the Commonwealth, commended the founders of the Greene County Historical Society for their dedication to preserving and promoting interest in the history of the county. The newsletters and magazines that the society has published since form the foundation for this story, which has been enhanced by the many artifacts, documents, textiles, biographies, and genealogies in the society's safekeeping. Additionally, the numerous articles that have appeared in the *Greene County Record* (originally called the *Greene County Register*) since 1903, including those about current events and repeated historical stories, have added to the rich mix. To the many people who have collected the history of the county and to all of the patient providers of photographs for us to scan and anecdotes, facts, and reminiscences for us to hear about—thank you.

The other members of the board of the Greene County Historical Society—Julie Dickey, Carlyle Hystad, Richard Early, Bill Jones, Eugene Powell, Joann Powell, Roger Powell, Cheryl Ragland, and Bill Steo—have my sincere gratitude for their encouragement and immense help, without which none of this would have been accomplished.

The space allowed for these acknowledgments would not let me do justice to all, and neither does the space in the book allow us to use all of the photographs that people have shared. Many people have filled in details and backgrounds about images provided by others, and I regret that your names are not all here in the pages of the book. We ask forgiveness for errors and omissions that inadvertently appear in the book. All of these photographs, and the stories that have been shared about them, will be archived at the historical society. We thank you all.

Many of the images in this book are from the collections of the Greene County Historical Society (GCHS) and, where possible, the name of the donor has been included in the courtesy line. The word "Greene" refers to Greene County throughout the book. There is no town or city of Greene within the county.

—Jackie Pamenter
President, Greene County Historical Society

INTRODUCTION

Some of the oldest rocks in the world appear across the landscape of Greene County. They are 1.117 billion years old, to be precise, and geologists call this kind of rock "orthopyroxene-bearing Mesoproterozoic granitoid gneiss"—more commonly known as granite. For eons after the rock formed, it uplifted and then was overlaid multiple times as liquid rock from the earth's core erupted, cooled, solidified, and was eroded. Eventually, the Blue Ridge Mountains were formed, and weathering exposed the granite outcroppings in the Piedmont that bedevil gardeners and farmers but are beloved by horticulturalists for the interest they add to landscape designs.

For many thousands of years before Christopher Columbus "discovered" America, Native Americans had traveled through this part of Central Virginia. The evidence of their passage and encampments is in the form of the stone implements—axes and projectile points, mostly—that have been found across the county. Most farming families have collections of projectile points, which have been exposed over the years as fields were plowed.

By the time the Virginia Company was endeavoring to survive at Jamestown, there were few native peoples in the area. In 1716, as the European population increased, Lt. Gov. Alexander Spotswood mounted an expedition with his Knights of the Golden Horseshoe to find out what was on the other side of the Blue Ridge Mountains. It is believed that they crossed at Swift Run Gap, which was far different then from the present-day smooth-surfaced switchback road. It is not known exactly when the hamlet at the foot of the mountains began to grow, but by the end of the 18th century, there was enough traffic and commerce in the area that William Stanard of Fredericksburg began to sell parcels of land in a town to be called Stanardsville. Stanard petitioned the legislature in Richmond, and on December 19, 1794, the general assembly passed "An Act for establishing several towns," which included the following: "That forty-five acres of land the property of William Stanard, in the county of Orange, as the same are already laid off into lots and streets, shall be, and they are hereby established a town, by the name of 'Stanardsville;' and James Madison, Zachariah Burnley, William White, May Burton, junior, Robert Miller, James Easley, John Beadles, Thomas Davis, George Argenbright, and Isaac Davis, gentlemen, appointed trustees thereof." Madison, who was appointed a trustee, was the father of the fourth president of the United States.

By 1838, there was pressure from farmers and other landowners in the western part of Orange to establish a separate county, partly because of the distance that had to be traveled over difficult terrain to the town of Orange for court days and other official business. The new county's boundaries were surveyed, and Stanardsville was chosen as Greene's county seat. William Philips, who built many of Thomas Jefferson's properties, is believed to have had a hand in the design and construction of the courthouse and jail. Stanardsville was the logical choice for the county seat—by 1835, it already had 21 dwelling houses, 5 mercantile stores, 2 taverns, a tanyard, a saddler, a tailor, a boot and shoe factory, 2 smith shops, a wheelwright, a hatter's shop, a gunsmith, and a physician.

Small hamlets grew up around schools or churches; post offices were established—as many as 10 during the decade between 1880 and 1890 alone—and often located in a general merchandise store. Greene communities were fairly self-sufficient, with Stanardsville being the largest. On Friday, August 21, 1903, the weekly *Greene County Register* newspaper began publishing. The first issue carried the banner "Subscribe for the Greene County Register—$1.00 per year in advance." Soon renamed the *Greene County Record*, the newspaper reported on local and national events (it included a weekly letter from Washington, DC), and carried much advertising. The first issue contained an advertisement from the R.N. Stephens' Store in Quinque: a "Mid-Summer Slaughter Sale" was taking place to celebrate the completion of a "commodious new store." The newspaper also reported a near disaster: "Mr. R.N. Stephens came near losing his handsome new store house last Wednesday. The lumber he was kiln-drying caught fire and would have destroyed the store house, if the wind had been blowing in that direction."

In the early 20th century, Sen. Nathaniel B. Early, concerned that the county would remain a backwater without better connections to the outside world, was successful in persuading the Virginia Legislature to route a major highway, US Route 29 (connecting Culpeper and Charlottesville), through the eastern section of the county. US Route 29's intersection with State Route 33 cuts the county into four unequal quadrants. The original road was eventually widened to become a four-lane highway, one of the busiest in Virginia.

These days, one could say that Greene is everywhere. From the late 1980s to the early 2000s, every CD player was playing music on compact discs that had been manufactured in the Nimbus factory in Greene County. Much of the agriculture in the county's piedmont is concerned with raising beef cattle for the nation's steaks and hamburgers. Other agricultural pursuits include wine production, as well as sheep, alpaca, and llama farms and the companies that process the animals' wool. Although the mountains are no longer home to the families of original settlers, the Shenandoah National Park and the Appalachian Trail provide recreation for countless visitors from around the world. Hang-gliders relish the winds that carry them off the face of the mountain so they can soar over the lower levels. These colorful "birds" would have astonished the area's earlier inhabitants! The same mountains contributed to our safety as the locus for training of US Navy SEALs during the Bosnian conflict in the 1990s.

Many of the photographs within this book are of families who were living in far-flung parts of the county; these images must have been taken by itinerant photographers. Photographer journeymen carried rolled backdrops made of painted oilcloth. They photographed their subjects outdoors, where the light was best, so it is not unusual to see a background of columns and draperies but subjects with their feet on rocky ground. Some of the most interesting details include the elaborate dresses and jewelry worn by the women, while smaller children are often barefoot. In the sweltering heat of a Virginia summer, women's neck-to-ankle garments must have been a burden—made worse by dark fabrics if the person was in mourning. However, it is clear that there was also occasionally more than enough snow to make a winter.

This book includes a few "mystery" photographs; the locations seem clear enough, but the people in the photographs—and the reasoning behind what they are doing—is not clear at all. These "mysteries" are so interesting that it would have been hard to omit them. Any help from readers who have additional information about these pictures would be much appreciated by the Greene County Historical Society.

One

EARLY HISTORY

Archaeological evidence suggests that Native Americans found their way here around 11,000 years ago and indicates that what is now State Route 33 over Swift Run Gap has been a popular travel path for at least 9,500 years. In particular, the area alongside Mutton Hollow Road, climbing into the mountains with some of the few flat and dry terraces along Swift Run, provides a useful stopping place before reaching the gap. Archeological finds of projectile points, corn pounders, and clay bowl fragments indicate longer-term occupation. It is easy to see how rock caves such as the one on the north side of South River would have provided excellent shelter during the strong thunderstorms that roll down off the mountains.

In the early 1700s, Europeans arrived, and they began parceling out the land. In 1721, King George I made a land grant of 24,000 acres to 18 gentlemen. The surveyors in the group marked the northwestern corner of the surveyed land on the Octonia Stone.

Until the Civil War and the Emancipation Proclamation, plantation owners and others used slaves to work their farms. After the Civil War, farming practices had to change, and they did; large plantations generally shrank, and for many decades a variety of crops were grown on smallholdings. Mountain residents harvested lumber, fruits, and nuts; kept a few hogs, cattle, and sheep for their own needs; and bartered for what they could not produce. Families worked the land together.

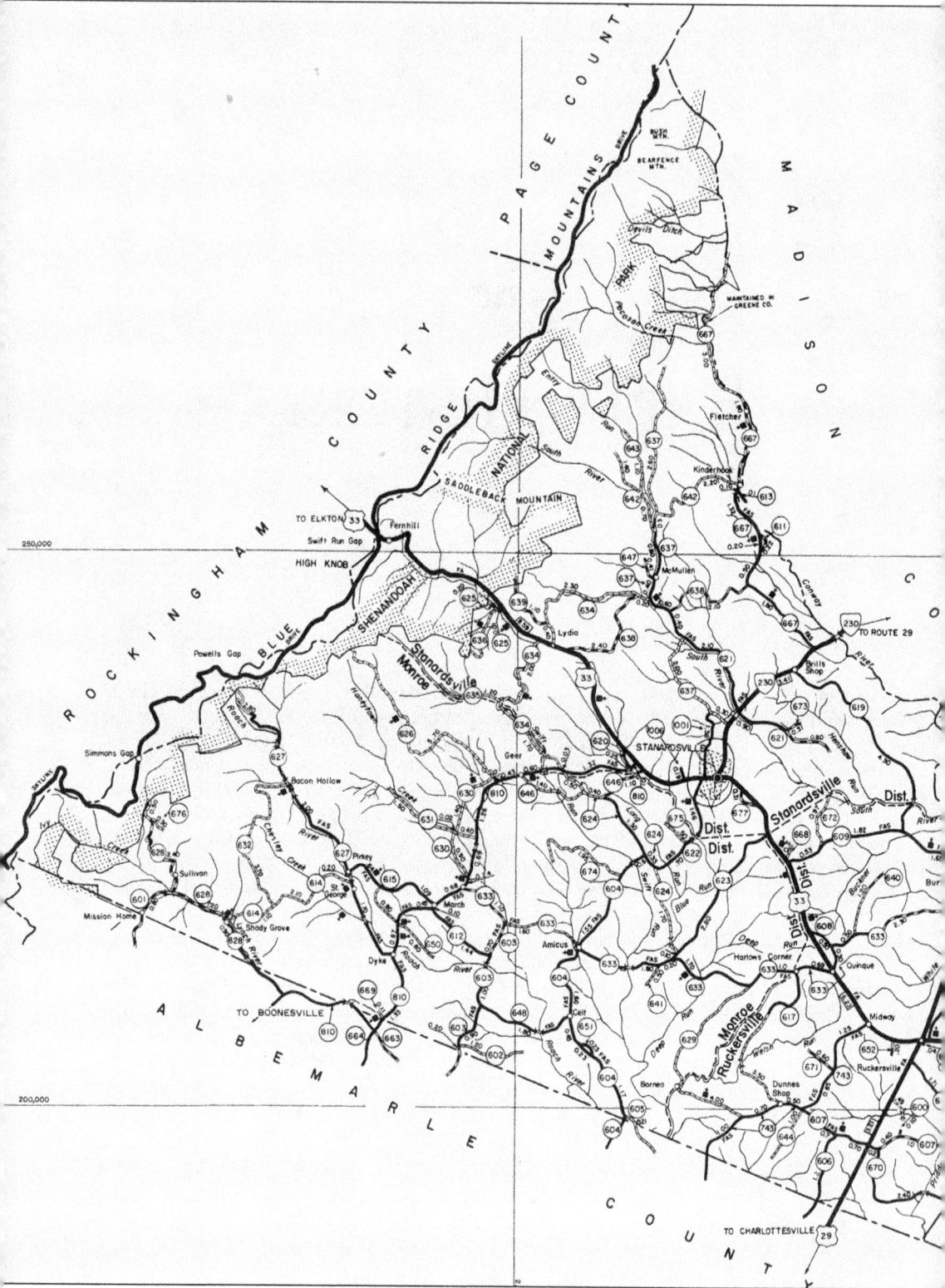

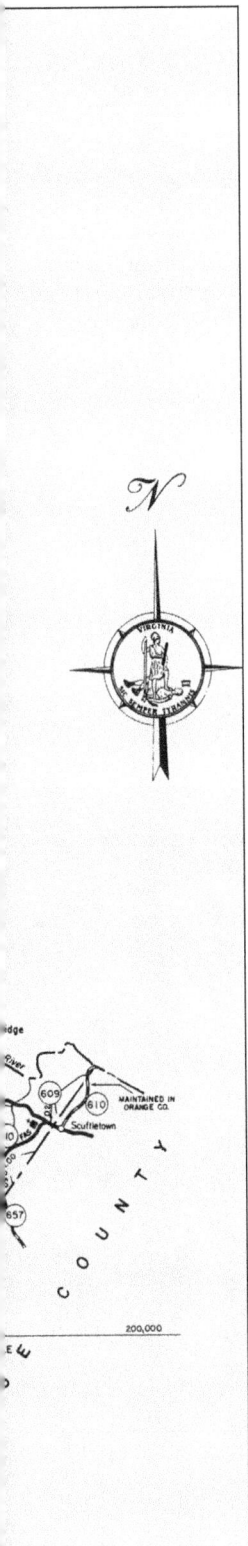

This 1975 map of Greene County shows the present-day major roads and crossroads and the larger of the numerous rivers and streams running east from the mountains. There are many differences in road numbers from those used on earlier maps: for example, Route 17 on the Virginia Department of Transportation's 1932 map became Route 33 by 1941. Earlier maps also showed villages such as Celt, close to the Albemarle County line, which leaves Route 604's name—Celt Road—as its legacy. The earlier map also shows US Route 29 taking a westerly turn where it intersects with present-day Route 33, then heading south at Midway along today's Advance Mills Road (Route 743); by the time the 1941 map was published, Route 29 headed directly south on the path that Virginians now know. (Virginia Department of Transportation.)

These projectile points and the square object come from the Mutton Hollow Road area along Swift Run. They were found during the 2005 Columbia Gas excavations. The square object may have been worn as jewelry. (GCHS, gift of Charlie Deane, except the stone axe, which is part of the Helen Hord collection.)

The Octonia Stone, engraved with two vertically aligned circles topped by a cross, marks the northwestern corner of the 1721 Octonia land grant. The stone is possibly the only surviving marker of the grant; since September 15, 1970, it has been listed in the National Register of Historic Places. (GCHS.)

During the Revolutionary War, Hessian soldiers from Germany were held captive in Charlottesville. Some escaped and made homes in the mountains. In 1825, one of them, a skilled woodworker, created two spectacular mantelshelves for the brick house being built at Lydia. This, the original dining room mantel, is in the home of Jerri Tata, whose ancestor bought the house after 1878. The intricate carving and original paint are unique in Greene. (Jeraldine Morris Tata.)

On the first page of the "Price & Hill Blotter No. 2, May 1, 1833" are several records, including: "Remitted our negotiated note to Garnett & Hill for $214 Payable at the Bank of Virginia at Fredericksburg VA." The book is a store ledger that was found in 2003 in the attic of a house on Main Street. (Gessner family.)

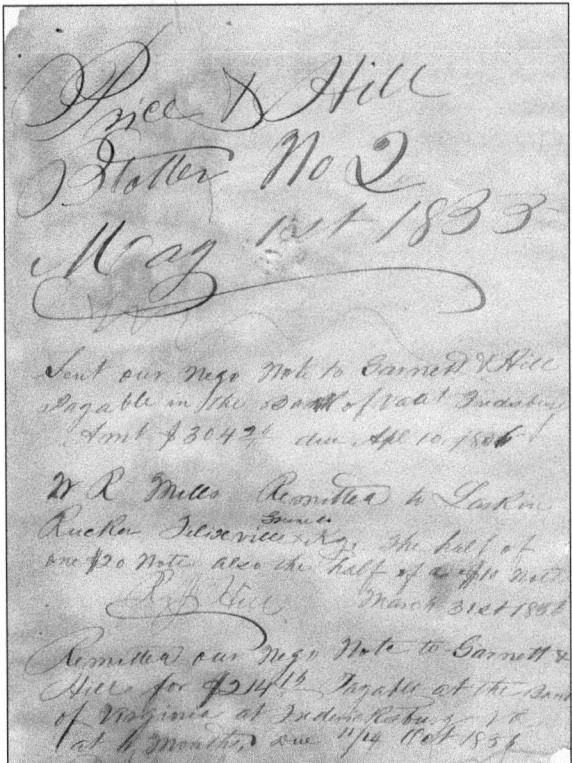

red Oak stump a corner of said ... 45 poles to the beginning ...

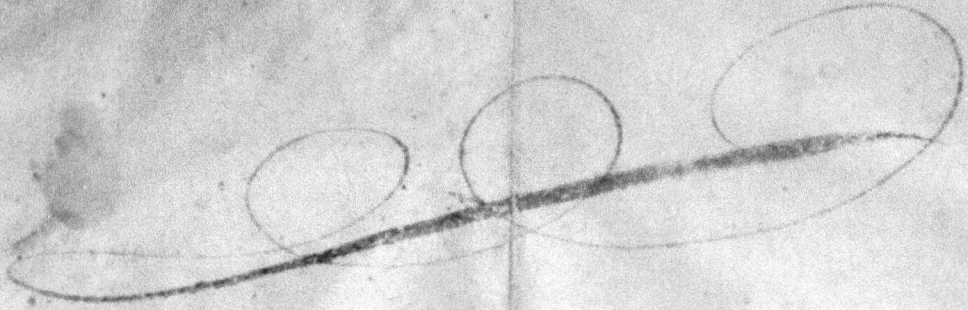

To have and to hold the said Tract or Parce...

Shiffalette and

In witness whereof

Commonwealth of Virgi...

said Commonwealth to b...

in the year of our Lord

Commonwealth the fort...

"On the eleventh day of November in the year of our Lord one thousand eight hundred and twenty and of the Commonwealth the forty-fifth," Thomas Mann Randolph, 21st governor of Virginia, signed this document, which describes a 43-acre land grant in the Dyke area to Overton Shiffalette, "near Delsmond's Old Line." It was recorded on page 466 of Land Deed Book No.

...and chance with his line at 36.6

...d with its appurtenances, to the said *Gratten*

heirs forever.

Thomas M Randolph Esq Governor of the

hereunto set his Hand, and caused the lesser Seal of the

at Richmond, on the Eleventh day of November

nd eight hundred and twenty and of the

Th M Randolph

69. The diamond-shaped area to the left contains the round wax seal of Virginia; although the surface color has completely faded to brown, it showed as bright red when the light of the scanner passed under it. (GCHS.)

This is the house of Capt. John Beadles, located in the Green Acres subdivision area of Greene. The land on which it stands was part of the 1721 Octonia Grant. There is a family cemetery on the property in which the Jack Jouett Chapter of the National Society of the Daughters of the American Revolution has erected a monument to Beadles for his service in the Revolutionary War. The original two-story structure was made of large hewn and dovetailed logs. The fact that it has two expensive brick chimneys in English and Flemish bond, rather than the more common fieldstone chimneys of the day, indicates Beadles's status as a well-to-do plantation owner. It may have been built by Beadles for his bride, Lurania (Lurenna) Miller; while their marriage date is not known, their first child was born in 1789. (GCHS, photograph from 1999 architectural review of historic buildings in Greene County.)

Today, Riverdale Subdivision marks the location of the land that William Monroe once farmed. For 17 years, he leased the 100-acre farm from George Taylor. According to an oral history taken from N.D. Chapman by Caribel Burke in 1999, what is known as Chapman Farm was built on this land by William T. Chapman in 1830. Although it has not been documented, it is suggested that the earlier portion of the building may have been Monroe's home. The part built in the 19th century was constructed by a local carpenter, Thomas Jefferson Bickers. Monroe, for whom the county high school is named, died in late 1768 or early 1769, leaving money in his will "toward schooling such poor children as my executors shall think in want." (GCHS, photograph from 1999 architectural review of historic buildings in Greene County.)

Many years before the map on pages 10 and 11 was made, this survey was conducted for F. and Valentine Winslow along South River. It is dated January 6, 1826—twelve years before Greene County split from Orange County. The survey, which refers to "Thornton's paper bearing date of 1732" begins at the bottom right (point A), "marked by two poplars and a dogwood on the north side of the river," at a corner with the Eddins property and continues along the river to point B, crossing Dundee Road. The river has changed its course a number of times, and the poplars and dogwood tree are long gone. Mountain View Baptist Church once stood on this road, but some or all of it was moved to a location on Madison Road in Stanardsville and became Stanardsville Baptist Church, which was consecrated in 1928. The Eddins family still owns property in this area. (GCHS.)

Two

RUCKERSVILLE AND STANARDSVILLE

Today, Ruckersville is the single largest "community" in the county, and it is possibly the earliest to be established, as John Rucker began acquiring this land in 1727. Ruckersville, which developed gradually after US Route 29 became a four-lane highway in the 1960s, has become the county's commercial center. In the mid-20th century, truck-stop restaurants flourished in Ruckersville; there was a jeans factory where the Greene House Shops are now located; and there was a speedway track that lasted for a few years. Although William Stanard's half-acre lots did not sell fast, Stanardsville—located west of Ruckersville—grew steadily in the 19th century, and by 1833, the town was bustling.

In the momentous year of 1838, the county's formation led to the building of the courthouse, jail, and other government buildings. Robert Pritchett bought lot no. 14, on which he built the Lafayette Hotel, which still operates today as a hotel and restaurant. Joseph Ham, a tailor, was in business on Main Street from at least 1856 to 1871. By the end of the 19th century, Stanardsville had developed a reputation for being a rough and tough town, with brawls and fights occurring on court days. Despite that (or perhaps because of it), the Bank of Greene opened in 1908. While many early buildings still stand, disastrous fires destroyed others in the 1930s. In October 1979, another catastrophic fire tore through the courthouse and other government buildings. Most recently, the opening of the Stanardsville By-Pass (intended to divert heavy truck traffic from narrow Main Street) took away much-needed commercial activity. New businesses such as The Standard Eatery, where Joseph Ham once cut waistcoats, show that efforts to revitalize the town are succeeding.

The junction of US Route 29 and State Route 33 looks very different today than it did 100 years ago. This photograph of the "Richmond Road" looks east towards what is now Route 29, which was built in the 1920s. A 1932 map shows the north-south Route 29 turning west here; it actually continues south in a straight line. (GCHS, gift of Jenelle McMullan.)

Powell Brothers Garage was started by Stark E. and Alton E. Powell in the mid-1940s. The building, located on US Route 29 in Ruckersville, was torn down in the mid-1960s when Route 29 was widened, but the business is still operated today by Stark's son, Michael K. Powell. (Roger E. Powell.)

This late-1950s aerial view of the traffic circle at the junction of Routes 29 and 33 includes many familiar buildings, but the circle has since been replaced with traffic lights. The Music Store occupies what was the restaurant (with awning, left of center), and the gas pumps are gone. The Wrangler jeans factory to the left is now the Greene House Shops. (Patrick Hester.)

The 29 Truck Stop Restaurant is believed to have been located just south of the intersection of Routes 29 and 33. These days, truckers use software and GPS to locate places to stop for food and fuel, but when this undated postcard was made, word of mouth was a restaurant's most important recommendation. (GCHS, gift of Roger Powell.)

Stanardsville Feby 18th 1863

Jack Blakey
paid cutting Jacket & pants   5 0 0

C R Estes
paid cutting Over Coat   5 0 0

22

Cash Dr To Thos Le Miller
To Cash in full

27

P H Miller
paid 1 pair gray gloves   10 0 0

Adison Powell
paid Mending Coat   3 0 0

29

John W Mills
1 fine vest for   50 00
making Coat   50 00
1 ½ backed Shirting   37 50
1 yd Sale linen   6 00
¾ padding   6 00
1 yd Cotton cloth   5 50
¾ Cambrick   4 50
1 Sheet wadding   2 00
¼ holland   2 00
Silk Thread & cotton 7 00 170 50

March 1st

Richard D Sims
Cutting Seary Coat   4 00

Mr Shiflett
cutting Coat   4 0 0

Joseph Ham kept a tailor's shop on Main Street in Stanardsville and also acted as postmaster and general retailer. On February 29, 1864, he recorded in his daybook, against the name John N. Mills, items including a vest, fabric, and silk thread. The goods totaled $170, an enormous sum in those days. That same day, General Custer and his Union troops came through the town, and it is quite possible that these items were taken as spoils of war. Unlike the majority of items detailed in the daybook, there is no record that Ham was paid for these "purchases." While Ham usually names his customer in the book, he records services such as mending pants for patrons listed only as "Federal soldier" in the years after the Civil War during Reconstruction. (GCHS, gift of Corinne Harris.)

This invitation, which reads, "The pleasure of your company is respectfully solicited at a Ball to be given at the Eagle Hotel (Stanardsville) on Wednesday evening the 26th Inst at 4 O Clock P.M.," was sent by Thomas J. D. Eddins and Isaac B. Davis, managers of the Eagle Hotel, to Ophelia Runkle on December 1, 1869. It is not known if she attended. Magnolia Blakey later ran the hotel; her 1925 obituary read, in part: "Not only was this a hotel, but it was a home for everybody from this and adjoining counties." The Eagle Hotel, shown below in an undated photograph, was on the south side of Main Street between Blakey Avenue and Ford Avenue. (Above, Jenelle McMullen; below, Booster Blakey.)

Tinsmith William Franklin Sims was born on July 27, 1828. He owned a house on Main Street where he lived with his family; his shop was open for business on the ground floor. He and his wife, Matilda Frances Creel, had six children. This portrait of William and Matilda is undated. Below is a photograph of an anvil and two hammers, three of the tools Sims owned and used in his tinsmithing business; they are now on display in the Greene County Historical Society museum. Among the items he sold were various kinds of candleholders and cooking pots and pans. (Left, Benjamin Sims III; below, tools loaned to GCHS by Benjamin Sims III, photograph by Bill Steo.)

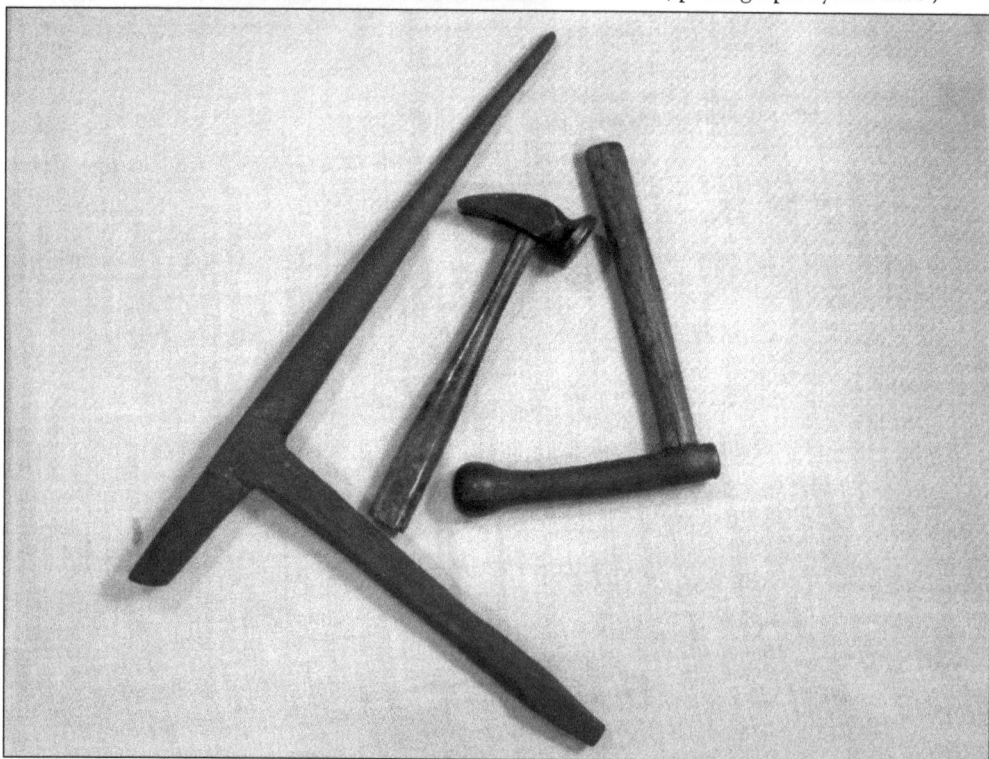

William Henry Brill and Mildred Ann Long Brill are pictured above in front of the Greene County courthouse and jail. This image is probably from the late 19th century. The Brills' home and harness shop were a few miles out of Stanardsville on Madison Road, opposite what is now the Greene Hills Club. Below, pictured some years later in front of their house are, from left to right, William Henry, Mildred Ann, William Henry Brill Jr., Ethel Pickering Brill, Anna Bell Brill, Frances Margaret Brill, and George Samuel Brill. Ethel Pickering Brill, who fathered 14 children, was known as "E.P.," for obvious reasons. The house still stands, but the shop burned in April 1939. The Brills' great-granddaughter Dorothy Bundy provided these photographs and the corresponding information. (Both, Dorothy Bundy.)

The Lafayette Hotel was built by Robert Pritchett, who bought the lot in 1838. It has since housed many businesses, including the Stanardsville Post Office. It also was once home to Stanardsville's telephone exchange. This photograph predates the 1920s addition of the second-floor balcony that wraps around the building. (Alan Pyles.)

This c. 1900 photograph shows the courthouse, with the county jail at left and the clerk's office at right. Pictured here are, from left to right, Mr. Morton, caretaker; unidentified; and Zirkle Blakey Sr. (both on fence); W.B. McMullen Sr.; Zebulon Kanky Page, county clerk; John Thomas Bray, commonwealth's attorney; Russ Melone; unidentified; and Reuben Thomas. (Julie Dickey, from the late Mrs. R.W. Coppedge.)

The property containing this house includes Francis Marion McMullen's Forest Hill Academy. Zebulon Kanky Page, then county clerk, and his wife, Henrietta, built the house in 1903; her sister built a similar one opposite the Lafayette Hotel. Z.K. Page died in August 1911. Before her death in 1935, Henrietta was often seen walking in her garden wearing the long dresses of an earlier era. (Don Pamenter.)

This undated photograph is something of a mystery. Clearly taken on Main Street, it shows a wagon full of men dressed in shirts and ties and carrying musical instruments. The holder of the reins is standing on the backs of the two mules pulling the wagon. This may have been a political rally. (Audrey Morris.)

This postcard of Stanardsville looks east toward the crest of "Town Hill," which was a favorite tobogganing place with the town's youngsters. Although there is no postmark, the card must have been sent before 1911, as it was addressed to "Miss" Henrietta Powell, who was married that year. (GCHS.)

This 1929 view of Stanardsville's Main Street looks west towards the Blue Ridge Mountains and shows the Stanardsville Post Office at left in the Blue Ridge Hotel (now the Lafayette Hotel). Next to it is the Golden Horseshoe Inn; the Eagle Hotel was farther along the street. This image was sold as a postcard. (Bobby Southard.)

It was a cold day when Jeraldine Morris (right) sat with her friend Nancy Blakey outside the *Greene County Record* office and posed for this picture in 1941. Morris recalls bumper-to-bumper traffic going through town after the Skyline Drive opened in the late 1930s. There was plenty of tourist accommodation—behind the two girls is Russell Powell's tourist home, which was opposite the Lafayette Hotel. (Jeraldine Morris Tata.)

Violette Price Moyer (1902–1997) holds a very special place in the hearts of Greene County residents. Miss Violette's Store, which carried practically anything one could need, was a gathering place in both winter and summer. After the death of her father, Thomas Price Moyer, Miss Violette ran the store on Ford Avenue (which he built when she was 16) until her own death. (Nancy Morris.)

A Chevrolet Will Take You There

STANARDSVILLE MOTOR COMPANY

We Maintain A Complete Service For Your Car   SALES   CHEVROLET   SERVICE   "Genuine Parts Used On Your Car"

STANARDSVILLE, VIRGINIA

DECEMBER 1955   JANUARY 1956   FEBRUARY 1956

SUN	MON	TUE	WED	THU	FRI	SAT
1	2	3	4	5	6	7
8	9	10	11	12	13	14
15	16	17	18	19	20	21
22	23	24	25	26	27	28
29	30	31				

PHONE 27

Wrecker Service — Day or Night

In 1930, Messrs. George Collins, Lindsay Bickers, and John Whitlock purchased land on Main Street at the foot of Madison Road for the showroom of their Stanardsville Motor Company. This 1956 calendar, which lists the telephone number as 27, still hangs in the showroom, which is now home to Noon Whistle Pottery, owned by Holly Horan and John Pluta. (Holly Horan and John Pluta.)

The extended Blakey family ran general merchandise stores in Stanardsville for many decades. This 1820s building on the north side of Main Street was home to Blakey & Company from 1930 to 1963, and the steps in front of the building became a favorite place for local men to gather. Zirkle (Booster) Blakey replaced the building in 1963 but continued to run the family business until 1970, when Blakey & Company became Greene County IGA. (Julie Dickey.)

Three

WAR

Although there is no monument to the Revolutionary War patriots of what became Greene County, 11 Revolutionary War pensioners are recorded in the county's first census from 1840. James Beazley III, Thomas Davis, Robert Holbert, Granville Kennedy, Michael Moyers, and Jeremiah Shotwell Sr. all served in the War of 1812. Many enlisted in the Confederate army, with most joining the 7th Virginia Infantry or the 4th Virginia Cavalry. There was but one clash on Greene's soil. The "Battle of Stanardsville" took place at the end of February 1864, when General Custer brought five cavalry units through Stanardsville en route to Charlottesville. After the battle of Rio Hill, when the Union troops retraced their route, they encountered 400 Virginia Confederates before retreating north across South River.

Of the 37 Greene men who enlisted during World War I, Willie Lee Morris was the first to enlist and one of three to die. The names of three casualties from the Korean War and ten from World War II are engraved on memorials in Court Square. Marine sergeant Allen E. Firth was the only fatality from Greene during the Vietnam War. Cpl. Adam Fargo, age 22, of Ruckersville, was killed in the line of duty on July 22, 2006, while serving his country as part of the US Army in Iraq. Other residents of Greene have served in Afghanistan and elsewhere in recent decades and are even now in harm's way overseas.

Many county residents work in defense industry companies that contribute to the safety of United States troops. Greene's mountains have played an important role in at least one recent conflict. In the 1990s and later, US Navy SEALs have trained in the mountains in Greene, which simulate difficult war terrain.

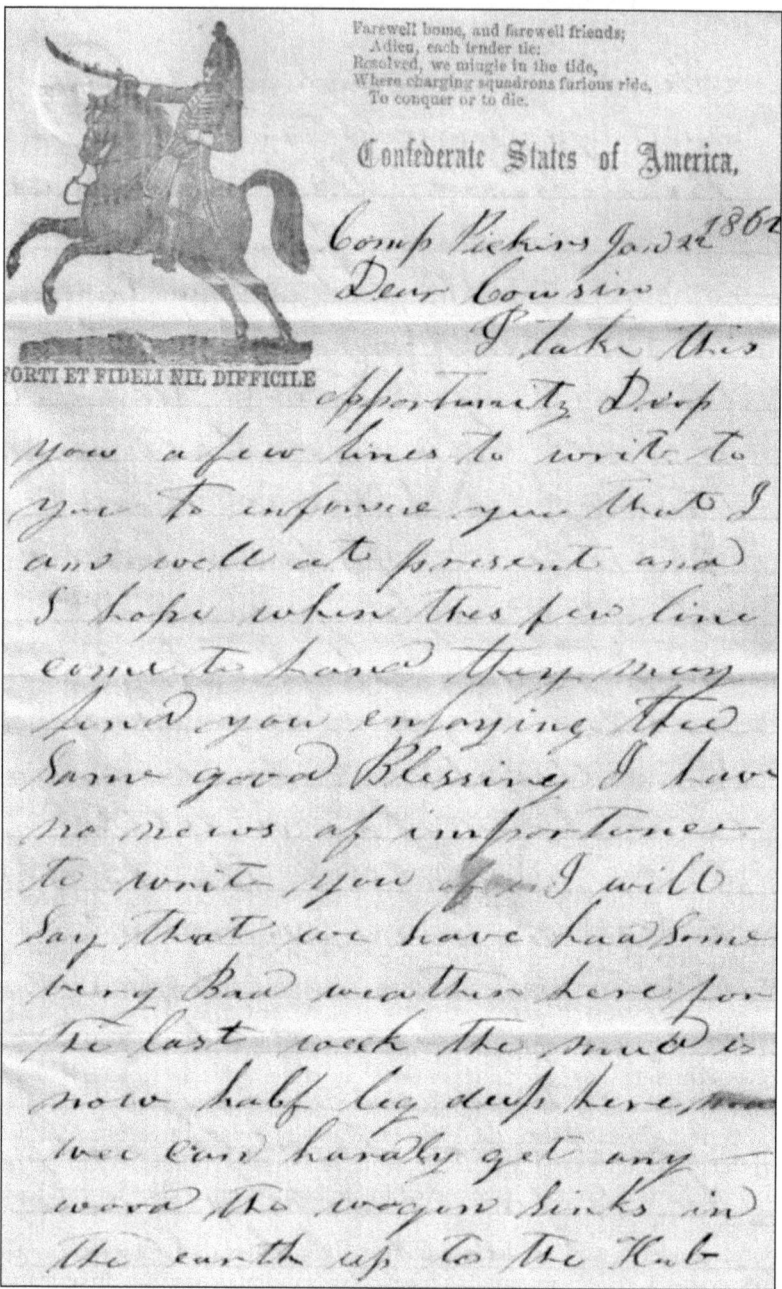

This letter from Milton Denson Lewis Runkle to his cousin Sarah Antoinette Ophelia Runkle (Phelie) was written on January 22, 1862, six months after he enlisted in what became Company D of the 34th Virginia Infantry, known as the "Greene Rough and Readys." He continued to write to Phelie throughout the war, as did his brother James and St. Clair Thomas Deane, who were also members of Company D, as well as James F. Finell; all of these letters survive. They were transcribed by Runkle's great-great-grandson Franklin A. Robinson Jr. and published by the historical society in 2011 in Volume 21 of the *Greene County Magazine*. After being taken prisoner of war at Appomattox on April 9, 1865, Runkle was paroled the same day. He returned to farming in Greene and died on October 2, 1918. (Jenelle McMullen.)

Jesse R. Pennington was a sutler who traveled with the Union army during the Civil War, providing food and other provisions to the troops. His dog (on the horse's back) clearly did not want to be left out of the picture. After the war, Pennington settled in Greene; one of his sons became well known as the county dentist. (Julie Dickey.)

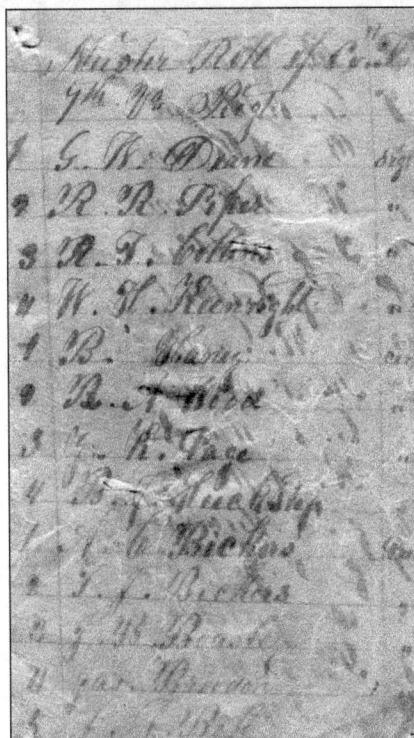

Twenty-eight names are recorded on two pages of this small notebook. This muster roll of Company F, 7th Virginia Infantry probably dates to mid-1862 and contains many familiar names: Deane, Collins, Haney, Page, Bickers, Beasley, Breeden, Desmond, Eddins, Gilbert, Herring, Jeffries, Jarrell, and Lamb, among others. (GCHS, gift of Ackline Deane.)

The marker at left stands near Shiloh Baptist Church in Stanardsville and commemorates the "Unknown dead of Ewell's Army." In April 1862, Confederate general Richard S. Ewell was ordered to protect Swift Run Gap during Gen. "Stonewall" Jackson's Valley Campaign. This required the movement of Ewell's division, some 8,500 troops, into two camps in eastern Greene and through Stanardsville. The commotion caused by this march down narrow Main Street must have been considerable. Some of the men fell ill, probably with typhoid fever, and were treated in the basement of Stanardsville United Methodist Church (and probably other buildings). More than 30 men died and were buried in the graveyard at Shiloh church. The photograph below, taken during the 1986 Battle of Stanardsville reenactment, shows an encampment next to the United Methodist church. (Left, GCHS, 2004 Stanardsville Historic Designation file; below, Julie Dickey.)

THE FURLOUGHED MAN A PRISONER.

Almost two years after Gen. Richard S. Ewell's soldiers passed through, Union troops were in town. The *Harper's Weekly* issue from March 26, 1864, carried a front-page article with centerfold illustrations of what is locally known as the Battle of Stanardsville, which had taken place three weeks before. In this illustration, which includes a caption that says "The Furloughed Man A Prisoner," one of Gen. George Custer's cavalry is gesturing with his sword to have the man in front of him taken away, while two women and a child have their arms raised to plead with the soldier. The accompanying story explains that the town's men were being held prisoner only temporarily so that they could not hasten south and warn Confederate troops at Rio Hill in Albemarle County of the impending attack. Custer's troops skirmished with about 400 Confederate soldiers as they returned from their foray towards Charlottesville. (GCHS.)

A second illustration from the same issue of *Harper's Weekly* shows a mill in flames. A 1916 obituary from Marshall, Missouri, for Chastain Garland Page tells the story of how he saw the newspaper in 1865 in Nevada. He had just received a return of $7,000 on a $190 investment he had made to fund a silver mine exploration. He recognized the burning mill as belonging to his father, Franklin Page, and swiftly returned to help his father rebuild the destroyed mill on South River. The undated photograph below is of the rebuilt Page's mill, with the Page home visible behind it. (Above, GCHS; below, Bobby Rhodes.)

The photograph at right shows cousins Buey (seated) and Phill Shifflett, who posed for a formal portrait before going to serve in World War I. Both soldiers were lucky enough to come home, as did many others. The three who gave their lives in the Great War— Willie Denison Call, Willie Lee Morris, and William Marshall Sims—are listed on the World War I memorial in Court Square in Stanardsville. This grave portrait contrasts with some images that soldiers sent home after deployment. The picture below, from the GCHS collection, shows three unidentified men with the shadow of their picture-taking companion at their feet. On the back of the photograph the sender wrote, "This is the best I have now but will have more made soon." He dated it February 7, 1918, and added, "lonesome as hell." (Right, Olen Morris; below, GCHS, gift of Paul Davis.)

This formal portrait of Clyde Sims was taken in France. The Clyde Sims artifact collection, which resides in the Greene County Historical Society museum, documents all the stages of his service in the military. After training at Camp Lee in Petersburg, he went to France as a veterinarian. His upbringing on a farm in Greene gave him experience in dealing with horses, which was vital to the war effort. While the US Army did not rely heavily on mounted troops, horses were used for pulling weapons, ambulances, and supply wagons, as well as for messenger transport. Permission slips to leave his post "mounted" suggest that Clyde was also a horseback messenger. The Clyde Sims collection includes postcards that Sims bought in France, as well as the American flag that draped his coffin when he died in 1976. (Benjamin Sims III.)

Clyde Monroe Sims's call-up papers, which told him to report at Stanardsville at 5:00 p.m. on June 12, 1918, state: "From and after the day and hour just named, you will be a soldier in the military service of the United States." Dr. E.D. Davis signed the papers. Sims returned from France in July 1919. He is buried in Prospect Hill Cemetery in Front Royal, Virginia. (Benjamin Sims III.)

This portrait of Mabel Morris Rice with her family gives no hint that she served her country during World War I. She was among several hundred female military employees who became known as "Yeomanettes," processing the great volume of paperwork generated by the war effort. Mabel worked at the Navy Yard in Washington, DC. She married Jack Rice in 1922. Pictured here are, from left to right, Paul, Mabel, Kenneth, Austin, Jack, and Charles. (Olen Morris.)

Norman W. Morris (center) was the first soldier from Greene County to serve in World War II; he was a cargo plane inspector. This photograph may be from the Army Air Corps base in Sioux City or from elsewhere in South Dakota. Morris was discharged with the rank of sergeant on September 8, 1945. The other two soldiers are unidentified. (GCHS, gift of Ellen Morris Deane.)

Amos Hudson Collier (fourth row, fifth from right) looks out from under his cap in this formal photograph of Company 153 A-6, which was taken in November 1944 at Camp Peary, Virginia. Collier was 23 years old when this photograph was taken. (Pauline Collier Clatterbuck, Amos Collier's daughter.)

A	BASIC MILEAGE RATION	
	UNITED STATES OF AMERICA N° 378196 Y OFFICE OF PRICE ADMINISTRATION	
NAME OF REGISTERED OWNER		VEHICLE LICENSE NO.: 533
R. N. Early.		STATE OF REGISTRATION: Va.
COMPLETE ADDRESS:		YEAR MODEL: 1941
Ruckersville Va.		MAKE: Chrysler.

HOLDER MUST FILL IN THE ABOVE BLANKS BEFORE THE FIRST PURCHASE OF GASOLINE.

Rationing during World War II meant that coupons were needed to purchase gasoline. The commonwealth's attorney was not exempt from these rules, as attested to by this image of R.N. Early's coupon book. There were still shortages after the war; even ration coupons could not get sugar or eggs in Washington, DC. The photograph at right shows a note Julie Gilmer wrote to thank John and Genevieve Morris for their hospitality and the sugar they had sent home with her. She shared the sugar with her neighbor and wrote: "Bring 8 to 10 dozen eggs next week if you can get them." (Above, Richard Early; right, GCHS, gift of Margaret Morris Curran.)

Wednesday

Dear folks,

We arrived home safely but the traffic was the worst I have ever seen.

Thanks for all the food and for getting the sugar. Ruth saw us unpacking and wanted to know what we had, when we told her about the sugar she said she didn't have a spoonful, I am lending her 6 lb and am sending you two of their tickets to get

41

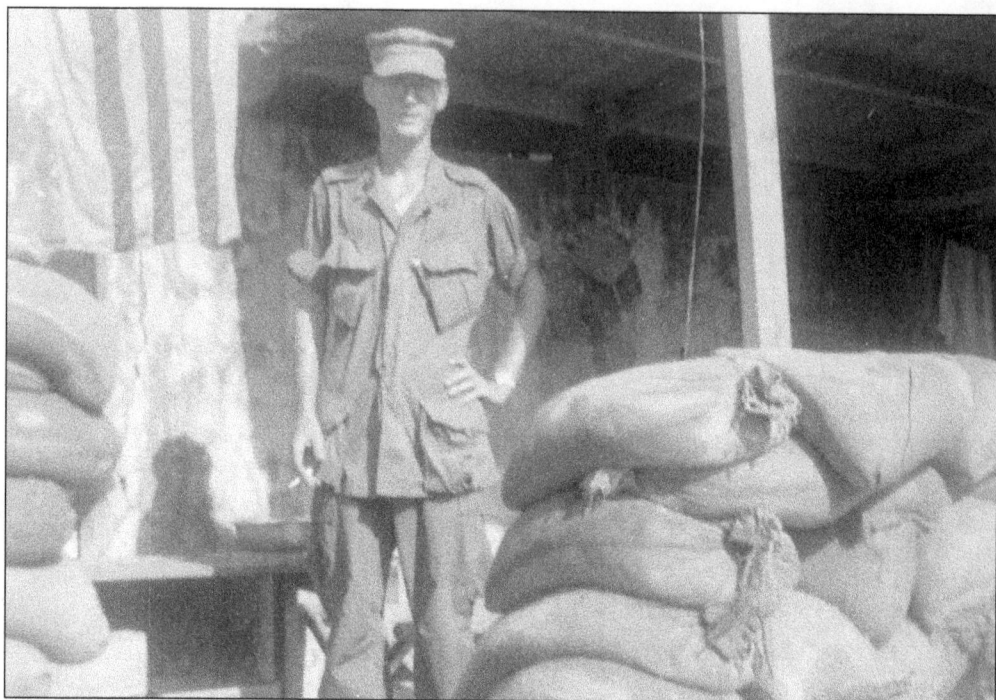

Sgt. Allen Edward Firth of Mission Home died on October 18, 1967, in Vietnam. He was due to finish service in Vietnam in February 1968 but was mortally wounded by enemy fire while carrying an injured comrade to safety during Operation Medina in Quang Tri Province. (Susan Firth, sister of Sgt. Allen Firth.)

Shortly before this mid-1990s picture was taken, four Black Hawk helicopters had swooped down on South River valley, leaving this group of Navy SEALs in a field full of cattle. It is hard to say who was more surprised by this close encounter—the SEALs or the cattle. The mountains of Greene were a training ground for preparing the SEALs for action in Bosnia. (Judy Braun; photograph by John Mitchell.)

Four

THE MOUNTAINS, THE PEOPLE, AND THEIR STORIES

Many of the oldest names in the county, such as Beazley and Powell, have been on property deeds in the western part of Greene County since the late 18th century, and people began to establish communities in the early 19th century. By 1931, when construction began on the Skyline Drive, there were several hundred people living in the multiple counties that would later become Shenandoah National Park. Pres. Franklin D. Roosevelt created the Civilian Conservation Corps (CCC) in 1933, and Baldface, in Greene, became the third CCC camp; these camps housed thousands of young men who would otherwise have been out of work. While major construction work was done by contractors, the "CCC boys," as they were known, built the beautiful walls and cabins and did much of the landscaping.

In the early days of the park, mountain residents were told that they could stay in their homes, but subsequent administrators decreed that nobody could continue to live within the park boundaries. Consequently, many people were forced to leave their homes and livelihoods, creating a legacy of mistrust for generations to come. Today, this injustice is publicly acknowledged, and hopefully, it is offset by the park's enormous benefits to all visitors—from families who come for a day to the through-hikers passing through Greene County on the Appalachian Trail.

The Blue Ridge Mountains are prone to sudden violent storms, as in June 1995, when 19 inches of rain fell in a matter of hours on some parts of Greene. The most visible destruction was that of the 1920s bridge over the Rapidan River at the Greene-Madison County line. In places like Kinderhook, buildings and roads were washed downstream in the torrents of water cascading from the mountain slopes.

The Powell home place, built in 1905, is located in what is now Farm Colony on Parker Mountain Road. The group shown is either the John Warren and Willie Florence Powell family or the Edwin Paulus and Bertie Mae Powell family, who moved to the home in January 1912; Willie Florence and Bertie were sisters. The memoir of Maudie Powell Haney, who grew up in this house, was published in Volume 6 of the GCHS magazine. (Bobby Rhodes.)

This early-1900s photograph shows Neilas (Cornelius) Shifflett (left) and his brother William Turner Shifflett (center). The other men are unidentified. The men were from Shifflett Hollow, where, at that time, getting around on the rocky roads often required traveling on foot or horseback. (Ivan Ray Sullivan Sr.)

Today, the Blue Ridge Mountains are densely wooded, but from the start of the first European inhabitation, lumber was a vital commodity. By the early 20th century, when this photograph was taken, the mountains were bare. In this image taken in winter from the southeast, Flattop Mountain is easily recognized by its shape. (Blue Ridge School.)

This early 1930 photograph was taken near the Conley family's farm on High Top Mountain. Pictured here are, from left to right, Blanche Morris Collier, Charlie Conley (holding Ruby Morris Roach), Elenor Morris Conley (Charlie's wife), and Zaddie Morris (Elenor's sister, holding Floyd Conley); Blanche and Ruby are Zaddie's daughters. (Pauline Collier Clatterbuck, Zaddie's granddaughter.)

An itinerant photographer at Swift Run Gap captured this image of Mary Rogers and Benjamin W. Dean around 1908. At the time, they were just acquaintances; Rogers worked at the Haney house shown on the opposite page. They eventually married and raised a family, living near Cecil Mission Church on State Route 33 near the Shenandoah National Park boundary. (Clara Dean Herring, the Deans' daughter.)

This early 1900s portrait of the George Austin Morris and Susan Clementine Shifflett Morris family includes, from left to right: (first row) Sylvester, Leviston, Ida, Susan Clementine, Francis Monroe, Altie, and John Paul; (second row) Julia Catherine, Columbus, Eveline, Willie, Mabel, Myrt, and Mary Ann. (Olen Morris.)

The undated photograph above shows the home of the James Alexander (Alex) Haney family, which was located at Swift Run Gap, where Haney ran the store and service station for travelers and the local community. The Haneys pose in front of the house with their three children. Teachers who worked at nearby Sunnyside School, which is shown in the 1925 photograph below, lodged in the Haney's home. Despite the heavy snow outside the school, there are at least six pupils on the porch, so the weather clearly was no deterrent to learning. (Both, Jack Hensley.)

In this 1930 image of Swift Run Gap, the Haney home is visible behind the trees at right; Haney's service station—with two Conoco pumps—is at left. The pyramid commemorating Gov. Alexander Spotswood and his Knights of the Golden Horseshoe, which is partially visible behind the Rockingham County sign, has since been moved to the south side of State Route 33. (Jack Hensley.)

Only three years after the 1930 photograph above was taken, the first three Civilian Conservation Corps (CCC) camps were established, including the one a few miles north at Baldface (NP-3). Al Green, who had traveled from Kentucky to join the CCC, took many photographs that record CCC life. (Jack Hensley, photograph by Al Green.)

Starting in 1933, the CCC worked year-round as men based in 10 camps built the infrastructure of Shenandoah National Park. While the summer heat was easier to bear on the mountain ridges than in the Piedmont, several of the photographs taken by Al Green offer an idea of just how snowy it could be! (Jack Hensley, photograph by Al Green.)

This postcard shows the Skyline Drive winding through Shenandoah National Park. It is undated, but judging from the state of the overlooks and the small amount of regrowth in the forested areas, it appears that work on the park had been recently completed. (GCHS, gift of Jackie Pamenter.)

Families who lived in the mountains harvested chestnuts and used the wood of the giant trees until chestnut blight, which was introduced in the early 1900s, destroyed these forests. The dead trees in this early postcard from Shenandoah National Park are a stark reminder of the disaster. The American Chestnut Foundation is working to restore the American chestnut tree to its native range. (Ellen Morris Deane.)

In June 1940, a member of the Early family took the above photograph of their outing to the South River Picnic Grounds on the Skyline Drive. The family was at one of the picnic areas built by the CCC boys a few years before; the picnic table would have been their handiwork. The photograph at right shows Robert D. Via and Annette Powell; it also shows the CCC's handiwork on the beautiful stone wall. After more than 75 years, the walls throughout the park were recently refurbished. (Above, Richard Early; right, Franklin A. Robinson Jr.)

Swift Run Crossroads
Shenandoah National Park

By 1950, Shenandoah National Park had been open for 15 years; automobiles were larger and more powerful and could take families on longer trips. The park and places such as Swift Run Gap had become favorite subjects for postcards like the one above, which shows numerous cars stopped at the service station. The photograph below shows Jack Hensley (holding a box of Camel cigarettes) working to unload supplies for the service station along with other unidentified people. Other establishments, such as the Mountain View Tea Room, catered to the ever-increasing demand for meals and also became the subjects of postcards. (Both, Jack Hensley.)

This poignant photograph was taken on February 24, 2012. Both structures are part of what was once the Madison Timber Corporation's lap (timber rights) on Willie and Edgar Lamb's property. The buildings, which have been reduced to skeletal remains, were probably a tenant-occupied dwelling and an outbuilding (most likely a corn house). With the regrowth of the forest that has taken place in the last 75 years, it is hard to imagine this scene as it once was: a home with a yard, a vegetable patch, and perhaps a flower garden. It is very close to the original road that ran across the ridgeline of Lewis Mountain (also known as Lamb's Mountain) beginning near the overlook at the Lewis Mountain campground and running to the Conway River. (Kristie Kendall.)

Even after the rain had stopped on June 27, 1995, flood water continued to gush from the hollows. In the photograph above, of Shelton's Ford at South River, the road leading toward the background forms a T-junction with State Route 637 at the striped marker drum; neither road is visible. The gate at left had been carried downstream by the floodwaters. The photograph below was taken after the flood waters receded at Kinderhook. This house was saved by the debris caught in the trees, which formed a barrier that diverted the water around the house. (Above, Bobby Rhodes; below, Ellen Morris Deane.)

Five

EDUCATION

Before schools were established in Greene, children were taught at home, which made sense when travel was on foot or by horse and buggy, and households hired tutors to teach all of their children. Eventually, farm families pooled resources, built one-room schoolhouses, and hired teachers for schools with names such as St. James, Big Bend, and Lower Pocosan. By the 1850s, there were also schools such as the Greene Classical and Mathematical Academy in Stanardsville. By 1886–1887, when statewide public education was established, 31 public schools in Greene served 899 white children and 265 colored children.

Some one-room schoolhouses are still standing today; others were closed when families moved from the mountains with the advent of the park. In the early 1900s, two industrial schools served mountain families: the Blue Ridge Industrial School (BRIS) in Dyke, and the Church of the Brethren Industrial School (CBIS) in Geer. CBIS included instruction in "trucking, barbering, carpentering, canning, washing, ironing, churning, pruning, shoesoling, mending, baking, sewing, playing" in its curriculum. In 1962, BRIS became the Blue Ridge School, a private boys' school.

William Monroe School was built in Stanardsville in 1926 and housed all grades of students through at least the early 1940s. It was named for Greene (at the time, Orange) County resident William Monroe, who died in 1768 or 1769 and left money to go toward educating poor children. After the separation of Greene from Orange in 1838, Greene eventually received a portion of Monroe's bequest.

Greene desegregated its schools in 1965. Until that point, what is now the Greene County Technical Education Center had been the central black school; students in grades 8 through 12 were bused to Charlottesville. For many families throughout the county, early education has come full circle as homeschooling has increased.

On March 31, 1813, James Powell signed his name after working through a page of compound multiplication examples in his manuscript arithmetic book (at left). It was a Wednesday, and Powell had just celebrated his 16th birthday; he embellished his name with some circles and lines. He continued to use this book for another three years. On the page shown below, an unknown student made notes about the denominations of "English Money": pound, shilling, penny, and farthing. Although federal money was the official coinage in 1790, English money remained in circulation, especially in rural areas, until much later. (Left, GCHS, gift of Lacuta Powell; below, GCHS, gift of Ethel Dillard.)

Francis Marion McMullan and his wife, Virginia, taught in Greene before and after the Civil War. He was principal of the Greene Classical and Mathematical Academy in the 1850s and early 1860s. After serving in the war, he bought property on the outskirts of Stanardsville to build Forest Hill Academy. The range of subjects was diverse, as seen on this blank monthly report from the 1857–1858 session of the Greene Classical and Mathematical Academy; they included surveying, calculus, and astronomy, as well as subjects familiar to present-day students. Joseph Ham, the tailor, sent at least four children to Forest Hill Academy. (Both, Don and Jackie Pamenter, gift of Emily McMullen Williams.)

GREENE CLASSICAL AND MATHEMATICAL ACADEMY,

STANARDSVILLE, VIRGINIA.

Monthly Report

Of

For the Month of   Session----1857--'58.

STUDIES.	WEEKLY RECORD.						REMARKS.
	1	2	3	4			
Defining,							
Reading Exercises,							
Writing,							
Book-Keeping,							
History,							
Geography,							
Grammar, Latin and English,							
Arithmetic,							
Algebra,							
Geometry,							
Surveying,							
Trigonometry,							
Calculus,							
Mechanics,							
Philosophy,							
Botany,							
Chemistry,							
Astronomy,							
Logic,							
Rhetoric,							
Political Economy,							
Latin,							
Greek,							
French,							
Elocution,							
Composition,							

SCALE OF MERIT.   F. M. McMULLAN,
                                                   Principal.

10 Perfect.
9 and 8 Very Good.
7 Good.   Tardy,   times excused.
6 Indifferent.   ATTENDANCE   Tardy,   times unexcused.
4 and 5 Bad.   Absent, times excused.
1 & 3 Very Bad.   Absent, times unexcused.

This portrait of Jeremiah Newcombe McMullen (1832–1909) was probably made in the 1850s or early 1860s. The original is on a large format (7.75-inch by 9.75-inch) metal plate rather than the more commonly seen small daguerreotype in a carrying case. On April 27, 1886, McMullen was superintendent of schools for Greene when he signed the receipt below for Sallie Early. She taught at Public White School Number 5, in the Monroe District and had submitted her report for April, showing 36 pupils on the rolls for the month and a daily average of 26 in class. Teachers' pay depended on the number of pupils they taught. (Left, Emily McMullen Williams; below, GCHS.)

In this c. 1912 photograph, the one-room schoolhouse for Kinderhook School is visible in the background. Starting from the far left, six of the boys in the front row are thought to be the sons of Michael Price Rhodes and Dollie Deane Rhodes: Arthur Cleveland, George Sinclair Sr., Percy Graydon, Velman Gordon, William Hobart, and Richard Whitelaw; also on the front row is Eugene Eppard and Teedie Deane. The woman at the left in the back row and the woman wearing a pinafore over a checked blouse are believed to be two of Hiram Franklin Breeden's daughters. Other people are not identified. (Bobby Rhodes.)

This c. 1912 photograph is of the Dunkard Victory Hill School on Cecil Raines' property in Haneytown. The few people identified are, starting at the left in the front row, Dennis and James Shifflett, (far right) teacher Ellen Wampler, later Mrs. Ellen W. Morris; (second row) Addie (second from left) and Annie Shifflett (third from left); (third row) Maidie (at far left), Mamie (third from left), and Douglas Shifflett (fifth from right). Leonard Raines, in striped tie, stands right of the doorway with a shorter boy to his right. (Karen Raines Callaway.)

The Parrot School was on the Amicus Road property of Bezaleel Brown Parrott, who was an early leader in Greene's public education system. His granddaughter Lucy T. Parrott, who taught at the school, is standing on the far right in this 1910 picture taken by Virgie Bell. (GCHS, gift of Woodie B. Parrott.)

James H. Sims was born in Ruckersville in 1913; he is shown here in an undated school portrait. A jack-of-all-trades, he became proficient in carpentry, masonry, plumbing, and electrical work and eventually became the first federally certified black electrician in West Virginia coal mining. Sims married Elsie Trice in November 1935 and the couple had two daughters, Betty Sims Brown and Peggy Sims Warner. (Betty Sims Brown.)

Promotion Card

South River School
NAME OF SCHOOL

McMullen, Va
POST OFFICE

This Certifies that Ida Breeden

has completed satisfactorily the Course of Study prescribed for the Fifth

Grade, and is hereby promoted to the Sixth Grade for the next Session.

_____ PRINCIPAL.

Laura C. Moyers TEACHER

General Average 94 Date March 17 1917

Published by Sheridan's School Supply Co., Greenwood, S. C.

Before Virginia had SOLs (Standards of Learning), there were promotion cards. Ida Breeden attended the South River School (also known as the McMullen School), and on March 17, 1917, her teacher, Laura C. Moyers, signed her promotion card so that Breeden could move up to the sixth grade. Many years later, Moyers (left) and Breeden stood for a portrait. Moyers taught for at least 40 years and Breeden for more than 28; both women educated schoolchildren across the county in one-room schools before moving to William Monroe School. (Both, Joann Powell.)

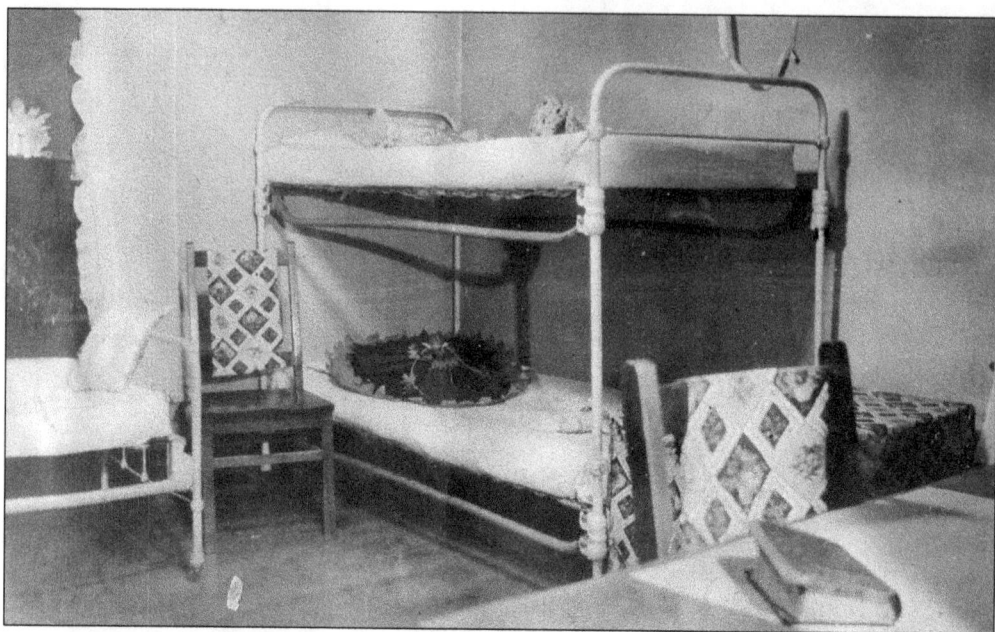

Many of Greene's students, especially girls, went on to become teachers and trained at State Teachers College (now James Madison University) in Harrisonburg. Jane Herndon, who recorded her luxurious accommodations in the 1929 image above, was one of them. Dolls on the bunks and a quilted cushion must have helped to soften the spartan surroundings and ward off homesickness. Herndon taught at South River School around 1930, where she took the class photograph below. Unlike many others, this was a two-room schoolhouse; the school building still stands and is now a private home. Herndon also taught at Ruckersville School. (Both, Judy Fitzhugh Estes.)

BLUE RIDGE INDUSTRIAL ~ SCHOOL ~

INCORPORATED

BRIS, GREENE COUNTY, VA.

(*The post office gets is name from initials of School—B. R. I. S.*)

✤

For Boys and Girls of Limited Means

Course of Instruction: Primary through High School.
Accredited by Virginia State Board of Education.

✤

Located in a beautiful valley in Blue Ridge Mountains, twenty-three miles from Charlottesville, seat of University of Virginia, and sixteen miles from Swift Run Gap, entrance to Skyland Drive.

This cover page (right) from a 1933 pamphlet advertises the Blue Ridge Industrial School (BRIS) as providing primary through high school education "for Boys and Girls of Limited Means." BRIS was founded in 1909 by the Rev. George P. Mayo, of the Virginia Diocese of the Episcopal Church, to help children of mountain families acquire a basic education and technical skills. At the BRIS Cannery (below) students learned how to process apples and other fruit from mountain orchards. In the early 1960s, BRIS became a boys-only boarding school and today enrolls boys from across the globe. (Both, Blue Ridge School.)

In 1922, the Church of the Brethren purchased Joe Harvey's property so that it could establish the Church of the Brethren Industrial School (CBIS). The photograph above shows Ellen Morris at the sale with her son Galen. CBIS opened the following year in the building shown below. Many children learned life and technical skills there. In 1934, the school was bought by the federal government when it built the Geer resettlement village for families displaced from the park. It has since been remodeled, trimmed of its upper floors, and is now the Rosebrook Inn, a bed and breakfast. (Above, Ellen Morris Deane; below, Shelviajean Allen.)

This June 1940 photograph shows William Monroe School, which was built in 1926. At first, all grades went to this school, but as the population grew, middle and elementary schools were built, and it became William Monroe High School. The classrooms were along the outside walls, with an auditorium in the middle. (Bobby Southard.)

Ruth Moore was a beloved teacher; this 1953–1954 fifth-grade class portrait is one of dozens in which she is included. The boy standing next to her at the back of the classroom is pointing out the location of Greene County on a map of the United States. (GCHS, gift of Marie Durrer.)

Cynthia Carpenter was born and raised in Greene. She first went to the black grade school, which was located where Greene County Technical Education Center is now, and then to Burley High School in Charlottesville for secondary education. In 1966, Carpenter was the first black female student to be admitted to William Monroe High School. (Cynthia Carpenter.)

This 1953 photograph shows the first four black teachers who worked in the integrated Greene County school system after segregation ended in 1965. Lucille McMullen is in the front. Behind her are, from left to right, Williana Scott, Alonzo Slade, and Evelyn Robison. (Cynthia Carpenter.)

Six

HARVESTING
THE LAND'S BOUNTY

Harper's Weekly, reporting on Custer's raid in Greene County in February 1864, includes a sketch of "negroes leaving their plows in the field to join our troops in the movement Northward." From the earliest European settlement of Virginia, labor-intensive farm work relied on slave labor. The 1860 census showed 1,984 slaves in the county—over one-third of the population. After the Civil War, families worked their fields, hiring workers when they were available. In an 1868 letter to John Henshaw, who lived in Kentucky, plantation owner Isaac Davis wrote that he would plant a much reduced acreage and might change to raising cattle.

Later, Greene's agriculture became much more varied. Long poultry sheds, used for raising chickens and turkeys, are still visible on the landscape, although they are not used today—new organic farms with free-range poultry look more like farms of the past. Farms in the mountains and the Piedmont still grow tree fruit such as apples and peaches. Making apple butter is a tradition that continues to this day as a way to preserve the apple harvest.

In the 1970s, Ed and Avra Schwab's Autumn Hill vineyard was at the forefront of the winery explosion in Virginia. In Greene, they were joined by Stone Mountain Vineyards in 1995 and, more recently, Kilaurwen Winery, as well as many grape-growers who sell to other winemakers.

The grist and lumber mills that were once in operation along every fast-moving stream have fallen into disrepair, and flax is no longer grown here and spun into linen. But in a new twist on old activities, the county has a fiber-processing mill, and small farms that raise sheep, alpaca, and llamas for their wool have joined Greene County's changing agricultural history.

Even after the advent of inexpensive cameras like the Kodak Brownie, photographs continued to be formal affairs for which the subject dressed up in his or her best clothing. Action photographs—such as the one above of Ollie Morris with his team of horses plowing a field—are relatively rare; the picture was probably taken in the 1930s. The plow in the image is little changed from the one in the advertisement at left, which was sent to James Wood in January 1898 by the Ashton-Sparke Farm Implement House of Richmond, Virginia. Wood married Phelie Runkle in May 1889, when they were both 68; they lived at the Runkle home place on Garth Road. (Above, Geneva Shifflett; left, Jenelle McMullen.)

In 1973, the *Greene County Record* interviewed Angus Gibbons, whose son Angus (Buddy) Gibbons, Jr. was photographed working on the Gibbonses' farm on Route 230. The haystack in the background was even then an unfamiliar sight—bales were already much more common. Buddy Gibbons was working land that his family still owns today. (James Johnson, nephew of Buddy Gibbons.)

Feeding the turkeys, at least when they are just poults, is something even a small child can do. This was probably an older sibling's daily chore. The unidentified little girl's grandmother is smiling from under her slat sun bonnet, while in the background, a piglet looks on enviously. The photograph is undated. (Ellen Morris Deane.)

No book about Greene County would be complete without some corn. "Indian corn," as it was then called, was one of the three principal crops grown in Greene in the 1840s. In this 1920s photograph, Bernice Olive Via stands next to the family car in front of a cornfield at the Via home place on Garth Road. (Franklin A. Robinson Jr.)

The mill at the Via home on Garth Road, which was powered by Swift Run, was one of many such structures throughout the county. The numerous streams coming down from the mountains provided constant waterpower except during the driest of weather. This picture was taken around 1932. (Franklin A. Robinson Jr.)

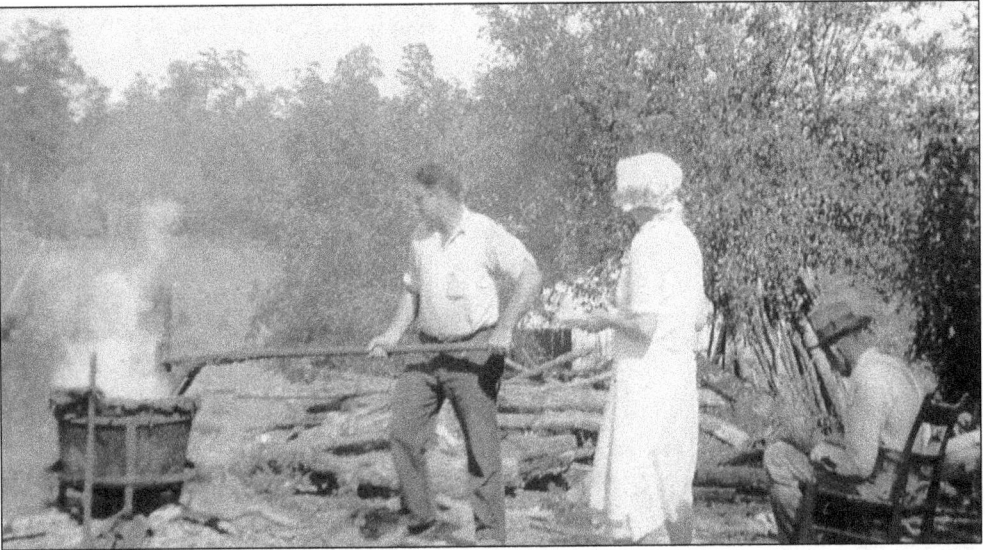

Making apple butter is a time-honored method of preserving fruit for sale or home use. The kettle must be stirred constantly, and a hot fire and long stirrer are essential. In this 1930s photograph from Toms Road, Walton Davis Wood stirs while Carrie W. Keyseear watches with plate in hand. The seated man is probably William Russell Keyseear. The recipe below, which has a typed date of 1944, is used by the Rhodes family of Stanardsville. There is a Rhodes family stirring poem that says: "Once around the edge/and twice through the middle/That's how you stir/the apple butter kettle." (Above, Cynthia Robertson Clatterbuck; below, Bobby Rhodes.)

Apple-butter 1944

1 sugar barrell, 2 large washing tubs and big gray pan full of sliced apples, stamons and black twigs. Put on at 3:0'clock took off at 5:45. 4 bottles of seasoning cinnamon and cloves and 100 lbs of sugar made about 37 gallons of butter. Started with three buckets of water.

P/S/T.

1 oil of Cloves
3 oil of cinnimon

1975 36+90

In this undated photograph, Roy Powell (left), Carl Powell (center), and Paul Powell show off their bird dog, guns, and catch. Every fall, brothers Carl and Paul would come from their homes in Northern Virginia to hunt with their cousin Roy in Greene, where they grew up. (Joann Powell.)

This 1990s photograph truly represents an earlier way of life. Danny Deane (left) and Brian S. Hammer pose with the results of one season's trapping along streams, rivers, and ponds in Greene. The pelts include beaver, muskrat, raccoon, skunk, possum, mink, otter, and red and grey fox. This was before coyotes, which prey on small mammals, became established in Greene. (Danny Deane.)

Here, Eley Yelpton Wood poses with his steam engine and lumber crew. Wood is the man in suspenders; his son Jesse Thomas Wood is standing under the cab canopy. The other people are unidentified, and the photograph is undated. Note the coffee pot hanging on the boiler. (Woodie B. Parrott.)

The unknown photographer who captured this image wrote this note: "I thought I would send you a view of Jessie Garth's saw mill, so you wouldn't forget how it looked. They are still sawing at the same place yet." This photograph is undated. The whirling saw blade is a blur, and piles of sawdust in the background attest to the amount of lumber already sawn. (Olen Morris.)

Some wood harvested in Greene—such as cherry, oak and poplar—is destined for a use other than in building construction. In this 1970s photograph, cabinetmaker Delbert Frey works on a table in his South River workshop. His son Randy carries on the tradition today. Fine woodworking, whether to make furniture or musical instruments, is still practiced across the county. (Randall Frey.)

Eugene Lloyd Eppard bought this Combine No. 62 from International Harvester in 1942. In the photograph, which was probably taken in the mid-1960s, Eppard drives the tractor while Walker T. Breeden is bagging on the combine. The combine was eventually replaced with one that automatically bagged the grain, making harvesting a one-man operation. (Harold Eppard.)

74

In this late 1940s photograph, George Marvin Powell, manager of Cloverly Farm on Madison Road (Route 230) shows his prize Angus bull Elenemere 1043. In 1968, this farm was sold to become The Greene Hills Club. Powell and his family lived in the farmhouse on the property, which is now the Pro Shop. (Mary Powell Breeden.)

In 1954, Steve Powell and his wife, Minnie, were featured in the *Charlottesville Daily Progress* under the headline "Greene County Powells Can Boast of Ten 4-H Clubbers." Here, their son Calvin Powell is working on his prizewinning 4-H hog project. Knowing how to raise prize animals is still important in Greene County. (Joann Powell.)

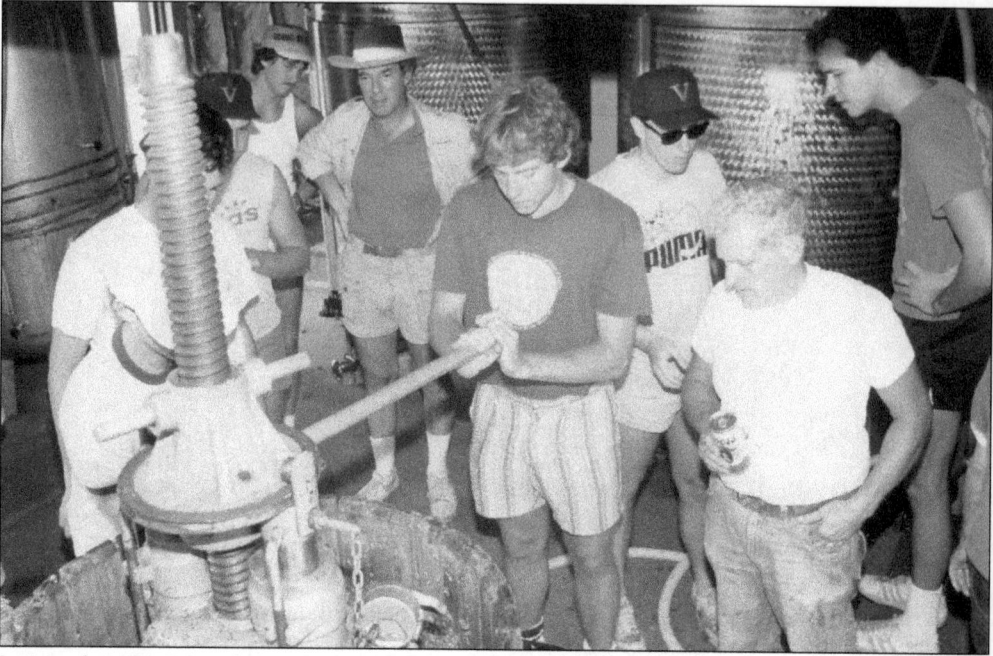

In March 1979, Ed and Avra Schwab planted the first half-acre of chardonnay grapes at what was to become Autumn Hill Vineyards. Autumn Hill is within the Monticello Viticultural Area, and these were the first wine grapes planted in the county during the current renaissance of winemaking in Virginia. The first picking and pressing of grapes at Autumn Hill (above) took place in August 1986; University of Virginia electrical engineering graduate students were enthusiastic pickers and helped with pressing in the winery's cellar. The winery sign was unveiled in 1987. (Both, Ed and Avra Schwab.)

Seven

CHURCH, POST OFFICE, AND STORE

Two of the first churches in what became Greene County were established in the 1700s by the Ruckers (in the east) and George Bingham (in the mountains). Many others, of all denominations, have followed. Some church buildings have been deconsecrated, and others have burned. Some are shown in the following pages. Those built before the Civil War often had a gallery for black parishioners. In Stanardsville, African American Baptists formed a separate congregation as early as 1862. Their Shiloh Baptist Church, built in the Carpenter Gothic style, was erected in 1907.

The post office in Stanardsville, established in 1815, was the first in the area that would become Greene County 23 years later. A Ruckersville post office was established in 1841. Communities grew around the nuclei formed by the church, the post office, and the store. In Volume 1 of the Greene County Historical Society magazine, Nancy Morris writes that at one time there were as many as 42 post offices in Greene, with each serving a hamlet or small community. Now there are just four—Stanardsville, Ruckersville, Quinque, and Dyke. Post offices named for the postmaster include Roudabush, Haney, Sullivan, and Lamb. As mail service was consolidated, post offices with names such as Borneo, Erald, Nimrod, and Pirkey were closed. The Lamb Post Office was established in 1894, with James Lamb as the first postmaster, but the postal administration changed it to Kinderhook 14 years later for the hometown of Pres. Martin Van Buren. After the name changed, the store became known as the Kinderhook Store, and the community around it became Kinderhook, too, with the origin of the name Kinderhook long forgotten.

The baptism shown in this c. 1905 photograph took place on the property of Edward Gibson on Route 627, with Brother S.A. Sanger of the Church of the Brethren performing the ceremony. Information for this photograph came from a 1986 interview with Maude and Pat Shifflett conducted by the late Mary Snow. The identity of the young woman being baptized is not recorded. The woman wearing a hat in the front at right is Molly Knight. It is known that Louvenia Morris attended the baptism, but she is not identified. While there are many splendid hats in the back rows of onlookers, the small boys sitting at the front are barefoot. The one squatting at center right and wearing a suit is Walter Morris, Louvenia's brother; the fact that Walter died in June 1909 has been one way to assign a possible date to the photograph. (Louise H. Sullivan.)

Brother S.A. Sanger is shown in these photographs from a postcard, which is undated; however, it is known that in 1898 and 1899, Sanger was a member of the Visiting Committee at Bridgewater College in the Shenandoah Valley. The college, which was established in 1880, admitted women from the time of its founding—it was the first to do so in Virginia, and this was a radical idea at the time. (Shelviajean Allen.)

Stanardsville Baptist Church on Madison Road was built in 1928. This pretty church echoes the Carpenter Gothic style of the earlier Grace Episcopal and Shiloh Baptist Churches. It is believed that wood used in its construction was salvaged from an earlier Baptist church on Dundee Road near South River. Additions were made to the church in 1956. (GCHS, 2004 Stanardsville Historic Designation file.)

The Rev. Frederick W. Neve, Episcopalian Archdeacon of the Blue Ridge from 1904, is pictured at left on horseback. Reverend Neve was responsible for the work of many missions in seven mountainous counties in Central Virginia. In Greene, this included those in Lydia, Middle River, Upper and Lower Pocosan, and on Wyatt's Mountain and High Top. The mountainous terrain and primitive nature of many of the roads in the early 20th century made travel on horseback a necessity. In the gathering pictured below, which was held on August 6, 1909, Neve is shown at Mission Home, standing out as the tallest man in the crowd. (Both, Blue Ridge School.)

This c. 1929 image is of Grace Episcopal Church, which was built in 1900 and consecrated on July 30, 1901, by Bishop Robert Atkinson Gibson. Rev. Watkins Leigh Ribble, who was rector of Grace Episcopal Church from 1930 to 1936, traveled into the mountains to minister to his flock in addition to conducting services at this church. (Bobby Southard.)

Joseph Garland Knight, who was born around 1833 and died in 1919, lived and preached in the Bacon Hollow area. In 1886, he sheltered two Mormon elders—Josiah Burrows and John T. Hales—at a time public opinion was generally against the Mormon faith. Mormon and Episcopalian missions in the Blue Ridge Mountains were still in competition with one another when Rev. George P. Mayo founded the Blue Ridge Industrial School (BRIS). (Eugene Powell.)

A homecoming photograph (above) taken at Shiloh Baptist Church in Stanardsville shows everyone in their Sunday best. These photographs are undated but were probably taken in the 1960s. A school that was built on the same piece of property shortly after completion of the church in 1907 may have replaced an earlier schoolhouse—an 1885 newspaper clipping refers to John R.A. Gibbons as the "first assistant teacher in the Stanardsville grade school" for African American children. Pictured below are, from left to right, Bennie Morton, James Mickey Sr., Phil Frye, and Albert Taylor. (Both, Cynthia Carpenter.)

In 1846, when it was first built, South River Methodist Church was closer to the river than it is today. In a talk given by congregant Ethyle Cole Giuseppe, she retells her mother Edna Lee Parrott's memory: "All the neighbors were there when they moved it across the road with logs under it and horses pulling it." The church was remodeled around 1900. Carpenter "Limpin' Jim" Harlow used wood from the first Methodist church in Orange (which then included Greene) County for the pulpit. At that time, the church was heated by one big wood stove in the middle of the building. During the 1995 flood, water ran under the church, as well as around it and in through the windows. The people in the foreground of this pre-1936 photograph are, from left to right, Harry Shelton, Tyree Sims, Monroe Shelton, Reverend Pullen's wife, and Reverend Pullen. (Bobby Rhodes.)

Liberty Baptist Church was formed in 1832 in the Kinderhook area; the first church was built across Middle River in Madison County. While the river there is usually placid and often a trickle, it can quickly become a destructive torrent. Because of this danger, a new church was built below Kinderhook—on the Greene side—in the 1950s. (Bobby Rhodes.)

This c. 1955 photograph shows Westover United Methodist Church. The church was built on a two-acre lot that was originally part of N.B. Early's Westover Farm. Construction was completed in 1913, with part of the money being raised by the sale of squirrel stew in the church lot. (GCHS, photograph from 1999 architectural review of historic buildings in Greene County.)

In 1894, the Evergreen Church of the Brethren was the first Brethren congregation to be organized in the mountains of Greene; the church itself, seen above in a c. 1950s photograph, was built two years later. By 1901 there were at least six congregations of Brethren in the western part of the county; these congregations supported the Church of the Brethren Industrial School that was built in Haneytown in the 1920s. (Shelviajean Allen.)

The first Geer Post Office was established in 1903 in a general store next to Mount Vernon Methodist Church. Subsequently, the building shown in the 1940s photograph at right became the Geer Post Office, with Loula B. Garth serving as postmistress for 25 years, starting in 1927. The man in the photograph is Loula's husband, Charles Thomas Garth. (Gwen Garth Conklin, the Garths' granddaughter.)

The Herndon family ran the Ruckersville Post Office from 1866 through most of the next 23 years. In 1947, the post office was still on the Herndon property. Pictured here are, from left to right, postmistress Lottie Herndon, Arden Harris, Mary Elizabeth Featherstone, and Luna Herndon. (Arden Harris Coulsby, niece of Lottie Herndon.)

Eddie Lee Southard was postmaster in Stanardsville from May 1934 until he retired at the end of 1958. During Southard's tenure, the post office was next to Blakey's Store on the north side of Main Street. In this undated photograph, Southard is seen lowering the flag at the end of a day's work. (Bobby Southard.)

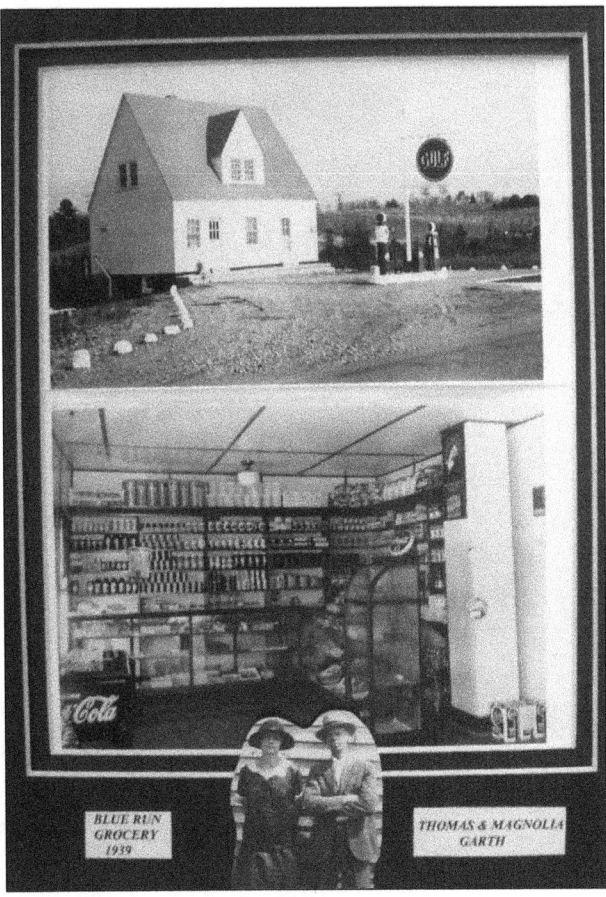

In the 19th century and earlier, the general store was often many other things, including serving as a post office. Joseph Ham was Stanardsville's postmaster from 1865 to 1871. His sign said "Joseph Ham Tailor," but this invoice, begun in 1850 and finally settled in 1861, was for dentistry—extractions, "destroying nerves," and filling cavities. (GCHS.)

The Blue Run Grocery has been a State Route 33 stopping point west of Stanardsville since 1939. Thomas Lawson, neighbor, remembers helping to build the store as a teenager, a job that involved hauling rocks for the foundation as well as changing the course of the river at that point. Thomas and Magnolia Garth ran the store; this montage still hangs there today. (Thomas Michael Garth, photograph by Bill Steo.)

The W.F. Morris Store at Geer on Route 810 was built around 1900. It was an essential part of life for mountain families. During the Depression, the store acted as a Federal Emergency Relief agent, fulfilling orders for items such as boots, clothing, and food for those in need of assistance. (Ellen Morris Deane.)

This undated photograph is of Sally Bell Gibbons, the daughter of Robert Angus and Fannie Lewis Gibbons, who was born around 1910. For decades, Sally's store was a regular stop for people living near Stanardsville on the Madison side of town. (James Johnson, nephew of Sally Gibbons.)

Eight

LEISURE TIME

Greene County has a long history of playing baseball—the Stanardsville Biscuit Cutters were a serious team in 1918–1919. After the Redbirds of the early 1940s came the Eagles in the late 1940s and early 1950s. By 1971, writers in the *Greene County Record* were bemoaning the lack of baseball enthusiasm in William Monroe High School. But what goes around comes around, and in 2012, the William Monroe Dragons won the state baseball championship held in Salem, Virginia. The final game was on graduation day in Stanardsville, where the class of 2012 became the first students to receive their diplomas at the high school's newly refurbished athletic facility.

Few know that Stanardsville was once a hotbed of marbles-playing rivalry among adults, with a corner of Ford Avenue and Court Square serving as the venue for fierce competition. Enthusiasts for noisier sports involving hot rods and souped-up automobiles could go to the racing circuit in Ruckersville in the 1960s, but it has long since disappeared.

In the 1930s, despite the Depression, people flocked to Stanardsville to spend a few pennies at one of Stanardsville's two movie houses. However, people most often created their own entertainment, and music-making was a key element of year-round pleasure. There are many local bands in Greene County, some of which include four generations of a single family. Perhaps the best known of the county's musicians in the 1920s were Bela Lam and The Greene County Singers, who were both recorded and filmed. The county still boasts several groups who sing at concerts and sell recordings, while others play for their own enjoyment—perhaps the music is in the mountains.

These photographs were taken in 1911 or 1912. The photograph above shows Ada Durrette Davis and Thomas Burruss Pennington Davis astride a horse much larger than the two children, with their grandfather, Dr. Ross Benton Pennington, behind them. The building in the background has siding in the traditional board and batten style. Pennington had a mountain farm where the family would go in the summer. The photograph below was taken perhaps a year later and features a different means of transport. Standing behind the two children are, from left to right, two unidentified, Dr. Pennington, and Minnie P. Davis. (Both, Julie Davis Dickey.)

This early 1920s photograph captures a group of laughing children on the porch of the R.N. Stephens store in Quinque. From left to right are, three unidentified, Lorraine "Plum" Delaney, Pearl Iris Watson Robertson, Carrie Lee Watson Copsey, and unidentified. A store—the Pic N Pac—still operates in this location, but the building shown here succumbed to fire. (Cynthia Robertson Clatterbuck.)

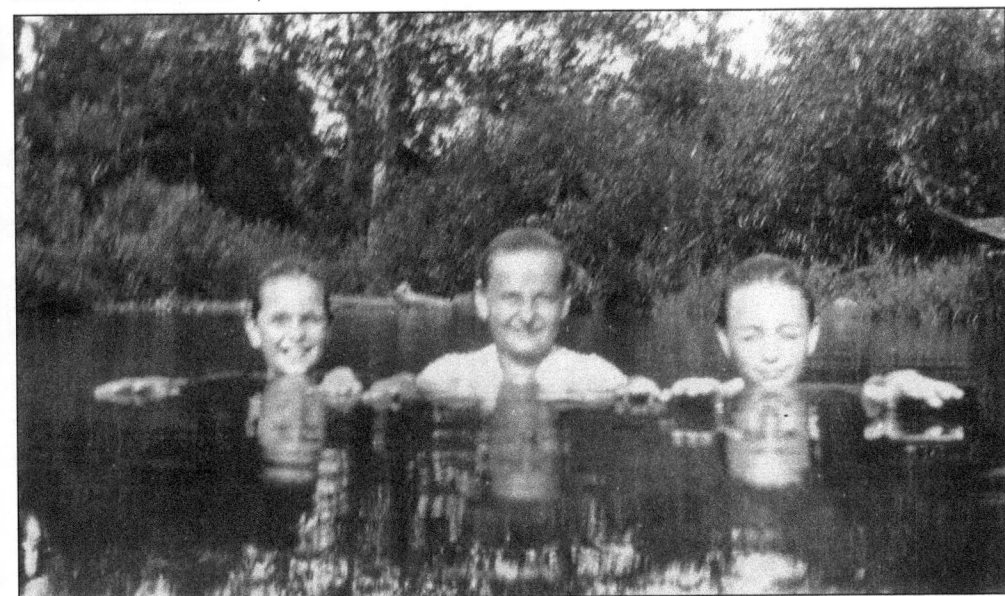

This undated photograph could have been taken in numerous places around the county. There are still swimming holes wherever ingenuity and a stream or pond will allow. These people are trying to keep cool on a hot summer's day. If they were lucky, their dip was followed by scoops of homemade peach ice cream. (Ellen Morris Deane.)

vantage of exercising the right side of the body much more than the left, and thus in some cases producing a slight deviation from perfect symmetry.

Value of Rowing.

Rowing, or rather sculling, is perhaps the most perfect form of exercise for young men and girls, for nearly all the muscles of the body are brought into play, with the exception of those passing from the front of the chest to the arm. In young persons with a tendency to phthisis or asthma I have many

Place yourself on the bars as in the figure, then loosen the hold of the hands and spring forward a few inches, thus moving from one end of the bars to the other.

times seen sculling effect a complete cure. During the period of adolescence gymnastics under a competent instructor are often of the most signal service, especially to young people who are naturally awkward or otherwise physically backward.

I need not dwell on the necessity of exercise for women further than to say that competent authorities look upon it as the best safeguard against certain diseases peculiar to their sex, the enormous prevalence of which at the present day is no doubt in great measure due to the physical indolence which many of them have been taught to consider as a grace rather than a defect—I had almost said a vice. In view of this it is

a sign of the times that the Ladies' Berkeley Athletic Club, in New York, became a flourishing "institution" in one year. I may say here that I think it is a mistake for women to aim directly at the development of muscle. The Venus of Milo, not the half masculine Amazon, must always be the type of physical perfection for them. Their exercise should therefore be chiefly hygienic rather than athletic.

Sports for Girls.

A great French anatomist, Cruveilhier, was ungallant enough to say that whatever women might learn to do they never could succeed in running gracefully. Candor compels me to say that I think the indict-

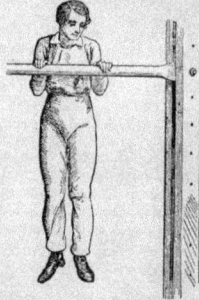

Place the hands on the bar, and raise and lower the body, bringing the bar across the chest; repeat only a few times.

ment true, but that and throwing the ball are about the only things which they cannot do with twice the grace and nearly all the strength of men.

One cannot expect under the storm and stress of active life to maintain his "condition;" he must be satisfied with having laid

In June 1900, 17-year-old Alma Shelton's father, George, gave her a copy of *The Golden Manual, or The Royal Road to Success*, which was published in 1891. It included the page at left, which includes, under the heading "Sports for Girls": "whatever women might learn to do they never could succeed in running gracefully." The 1938 basketball team in the photograph below would probably take exception to that. Pictured are, from left to right, (first row) Francis Blakey, Frances Melone, and Mary Lamb Dudding; (second row) Marjorie Parrott, Elsie Shifflett, Madge Haney, Charlotte Collier, Renee Cole, Elizabeth Early, and Phyllis Teed. (Left, GCHS, gift of Marian Durrer; below, Joann Powell.)

This image captures a summer outing in 1923. Pictured are, from left to right, Beck Douglas, Pansy Miller, Jane Herndon, Peachy Miller, and Elizabeth Durrett. Herndon later married Edwin Fletcher Fitzhugh; the couple had two children, Judy Fitzhugh (Estes) and Rocky Fitzhugh. (Judy Fitzhugh Estes.)

In the 1940s, Greene County's baseball team was the Redbirds. The team's baseball diamond was in the present-day location of William Monroe High School. Pickup games were a frequent occurrence—this group includes, from left to right, (first row) Dick Taylor, George Tommy Lamb, Buddy Southard, Clifton Lamb, Bruce Estes, Elliott Gilbert and Jessie Harlow; (second row) Dick Harlow, two unidentified, and B. Snow. (Joann Powell.)

These 1943–1944 team portraits appeared in the *Trail*, the William Monroe High School magazine. In the basketball team picture above are, from left to right, coach J.R. Breeden, Shirley Collier, Orman Marshall, Howard Morris, Zirkle Blakey, Y.C. Blakey, E.C. Gilbert Jr., and Billy Whitlock. Some of these boys played on the baseball team, too. In the baseball team photograph below are, from left to right, (first row) Max Oliver, Randolph Southard, Orman Marshall, Y.C. Blakey, Zirkle Blakey, and E.C. Gilbert Jr.; (second row) coach J.R. Breeden, Shirley Collier, Leary Knighton, Willard Lamm, Howard Morris, Billy Whitlock, and Hugh Garth. (Above, Pamela B. West; below, Bobby Southard.)

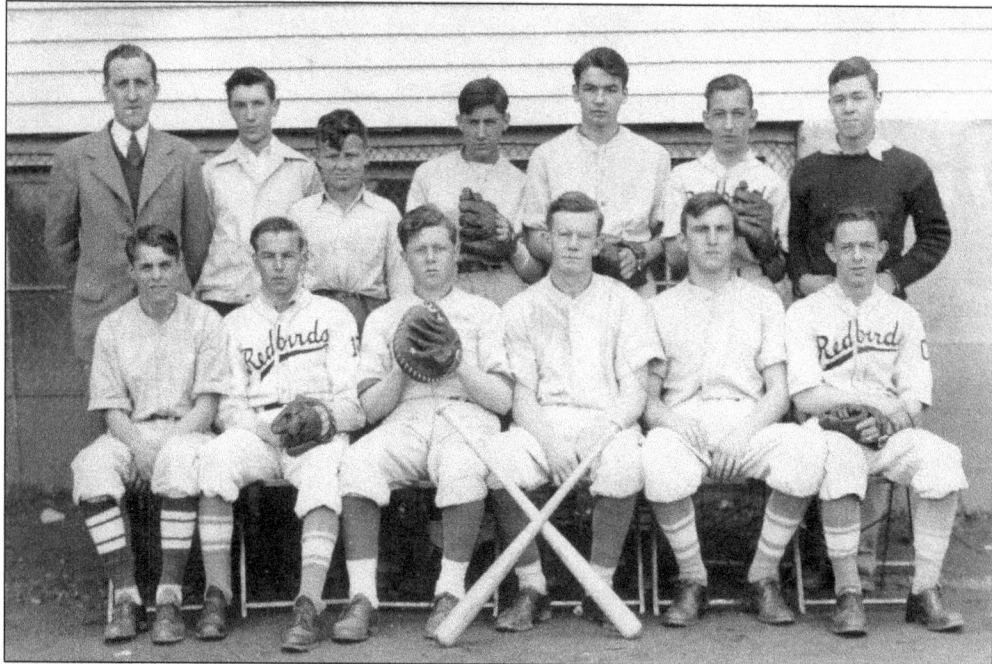

Pictured in this early-1950s photograph of the Eagles baseball team are, from left to right, (first row) Melvin Breeden, Buddy Eddins, Bobby Southard, unidentified, Thomas Garth, and Doyle Dawson; (second row) Dick Taylor, Buddy Southard, Thomas Lawson, Jesse Harlow, Milton Breeden; (third row) Willard Lawson and Harold Deane. Ray Snow, Sherman Garth, and Marshal Watson are not pictured but also played for the Eagles. (Thomas Lawson.)

By 1966, many of Greene County's baseball enthusiasts were coaching Little League. This Orioles team photograph includes, from left to right, (first row) Mike Snow, Sidney Trimmer, and Mike Berry; (second row) Kenny Shifflett, Steve Lawson, David Eddins, and Paul Lamb; (third row) Darrel Lawson, Roy Collier, and Ray Powell. The coaches are Willard Lawson (left) and Bill Trimmer. (Thomas Lawson.)

In this image from December 4, 1930, an MGM Lion promotion trailer is parked next to Graves' Hall, the silent movie theater on Ford Avenue. Kids and grown-ups crowded around the trailer to see posters, then entered the theater by going up the steps to the left of the trailer. Eddie Lee Southard ran the theater. (Bobby Southard.)

For Nelie Wampler, even recreation needed to be useful. She is third from the left in this undated image (probably from the 1950s), working on one of many quilts she made; this quilt was completed with her niece Leona Wampler (at left) and half-sister Pearl Wampler (second from left). The woman at right is Ethel Shifflett. The women are tying a colorful crazy quilt. (Ellen Morris Deane.)

In the early 1940s, Randolph (Buddy) Southard and his brother Bobby made a "bicycle built for two." Buddy (right), pictured here in his Navy uniform in the backyard of the family home on Main Street, is about to take the bicycle for a spin with his friend Hollis Jarrell. (Bobby Southard.)

In 1955, the Spotswood Trail Garden Club was pleased with the turnout at their flower show, which had the theme "Fall Glory Along The Spotswood Trail." In this image, club members Vera Estes (left) and Winnie Whitlock, both of whom won many ribbons, are admiring one of the entries. (Spotswood Trail Garden Club.)

These are 1950s photographs. Henry Lamb plays banjo with his son-in-law Bernard Shifflett on guitar (above). Sadly, Lamb's music-making days were cut short—en route to West Virginia to pick apples, he sat with his arm out of the truck window; an oncoming tractor trailer was too close, and Henry's arm was taken off. With a hook for an arm, he had to sell his farm, which eventually became the present-day Green Acres subdivision, and he was no longer able to play the banjo. In the photograph at left, Henry's daughter Lorene (wife of Bernard Shifflett), also a musician, poses with her guitar. (Both, Chelsi Smith, great-granddaughter of Henry Lamb.)

In this mid-1960s photograph, Mary, the ninth of Henry Lamb's ten children, poses with her gun. Together with other family members, Mary had to move from the family farm when her father lost his arm. She became a teacher's assistant at Johnson Elementary in Charlottesville, retiring in 2010. (Chelsi Smith.)

This puzzling undated mountain photograph generates questions for which there are no answers—who, when, why? The girl at left wears short sleeves, but the one on the right has a fur-trimmed coat and hat. Animated discussions seem to be taking place in the background. (GCHS, Galen Morris collection, gift of Ellen Morris Deane.)

99

On May 10, 1957, Norris Powell was Uncle Sam in the May Day Pageant at William Monroe High School. Taking his arm as Miss Liberty was his cousin Mary Powell. In attendance were "Indians" Barbara Haney (left) and another cousin, Joan Powell. The Uncle Sam hat, which is part of the Greene County Historical Society's collection, made another public appearance almost 50 years later, as shown at left in the photograph of Jeri Allen with Uncle Sam, played by T.J. Weeks, at Stanardsville's 2005 Fourth of July parade. Allen died on February 10, 2011, and is much missed. (Above, Joann Powell; left, Jackie Pamenter.)

Nine

CIVIC LIFE

Greene County's civic life began when it became a separate county in 1838. The courthouse and jail were built, and sheriffs, judges, and administrative officials began work. The first sheriff, William Parrott, served from 1838 to 1840; he was 84 years old when he was appointed.

After the Civil War, Greene developed a reputation for lawlessness that continued into the 20th century. Stanardsville could be a rowdy place at times, too. During Prohibition and afterwards, moonshine was produced here (as in many other places). The county sheriffs and deputies did their best to protect law-abiding citizens. In the early days they also had other duties—as tax collectors, for example. Even when this duty was taken over by the county administration, little of the tax money went to support law and order. Consequently, some sheriffs worked out of their homes and, occasionally, their cars; their wives might have been the ones to provide food for those in jail, even into the middle of the 20th century.

The Depression brought misery to many families; even though many grew their own food, stores acted as agents providing government help and bartered produce for shoes or other necessities. Tragedy struck Stanardsville in the 1930s when three successive fires destroyed many of the older homes and businesses. This was echoed decades later when the courthouse erupted in flames due to a gas-line leak during construction in 1979.

Throughout Greene County's history, people have answered the call when asked to contribute to the common good, whether as elected or appointed officials or as citizens, and this is still true today.

Thomas Davis was born on September 12, 1791, the son of wealthy plantation owner Isaac Davis Jr. of Locust Grove. One of the first public offices that Thomas Davis held was captain of the Orange County militia when he was only 20 years old. He spent a lifetime in public service. As a senator, he petitioned the legislature to create a new county from what was known as the "Upper District" of Orange County, presenting the signatures of 120 residents of the proposed new county; the General Assembly passed the act forming Greene County in January 1838. Davis died in his home on South River on April 19, 1853. This silhouette of Senator Davis is undated. The top hat he is wearing in the silhouette is in the GCHS collection. (GCHS, gift of Esther Davis.)

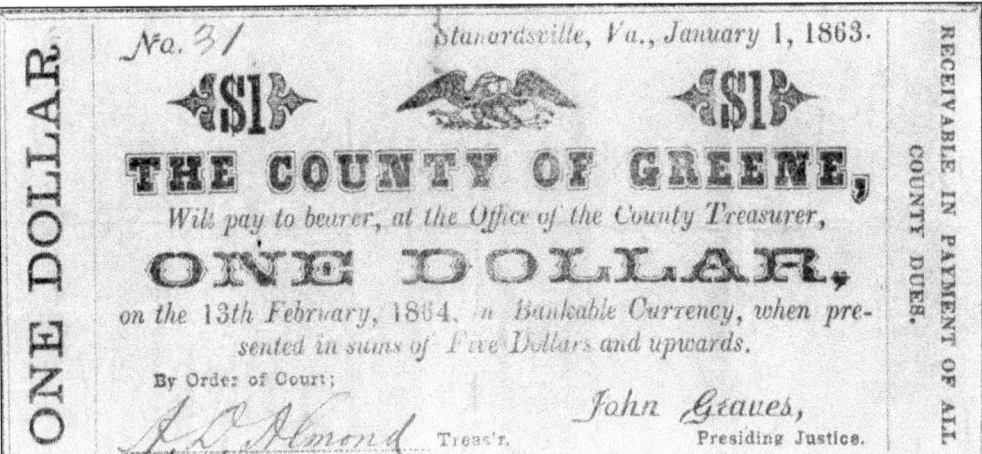

The note above, valued at $1, was signed by both Greene County treasurer A.D. Almond and a justice of the Greene County court, John Graves, and was issued on January 1, 1863. It could be redeemed for cash the following year but was most likely used to pay local taxes. (GCHS.)

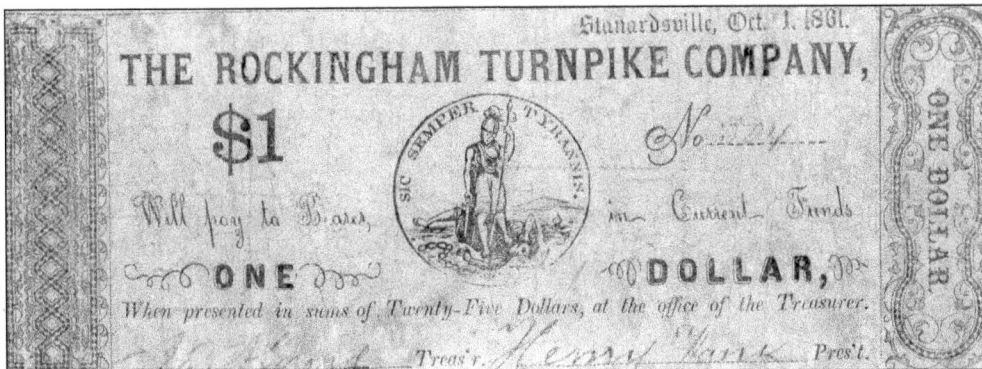

In 1850, the Rockingham Turnpike Company was authorized to build a road from Harrisonburg to Gordonsville. It would cross Swift Run Gap and go through Stanardsville. This turnpike, or road, would help get the Shenandoah Valley's produce to the train station in Gordonsville, and thence to Richmond and Washington. In 1861, the company issued stock in amounts including $1, $3, and 50¢. (GCHS, purchase.)

This daguerreotype of Maj. Benjamin Alexander McMullen was made between 1850 and 1860. McMullen was born on September 28, 1828, and died around 1891. He lived in the village of McMullen and was one of Greene's justices of the peace. He served in the Confederate army from 1861 to 1865. (Emily McMullen Williams.)

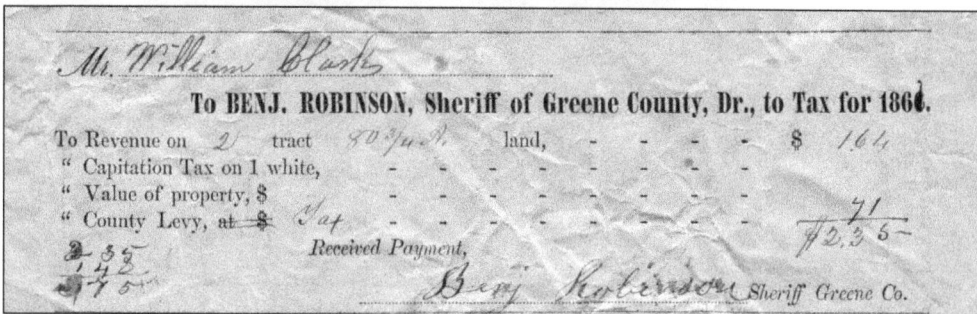

Benjamin F. Robinson was Greene County's sheriff from 1860 until at least 1865. At this time, sheriffs were tasked with collecting taxes. William Clark received the above receipt, signed by Sheriff Robinson, for $1.64 on 80.75 acres, plus a 71¢ "County Levy." The year, though it was sometime in the 1860s, is obscured. (GCHS, gift of Norma Collins.)

[For the WHIG.]

STANARDSVILLE, VA., October 10.

The colored Republicans met here to night to organize a Wise, Wood, and Blair Club. J. W. Coles stated the object of the meeting and made a very happy speech. The club was orga with Dudley Morton, Esq., pre A. C. Ramsey, Esq., vice-presiden. John R. A. Gibbons (first assis teacher in the Stanardsville gra school), secretary. The meeting very enthusiastic, and the secretary rolled 43 names.

J. W. Coles, Esq., offered the foll ing resolutions which were unanimous ly adopted amid rounds of applause: Whereas we, the colored Republi cans of Stanardsville, Greene county, Virginia, have seen the evil fruit of Bourbonism, and know that that part is hostile to the interest of the labi class of people ; and whereas the Re publican party has always protected the interest of the laboring man in both State and Nation ; therefore

Resolved, That we renew our alle giance to the Republican party and its principles, and pledge our hearty sup port to its nominees—Hon. John S. Wise for Governor ; Hon. H. C. Wood, for Lieutenant-Governor ; and Hon. F Blair, for Attorney-General.

Resolved, further, That in W. B. Gen try, Esq., our candidate for the Senate, we recognize a true and tried Republi can—one who has spent his whole life in tilling the soil of the "Old Dominion," and who doubtless knows how to sym pathize with the laboring man. In Cap tain John C. Sims, our candidate for the House of Delegates, we find a man who has ever been true to his principles. Being identified with the farming inter est of this people, a practical and suc cessful farmer, he necessarily knows the needs of the laboring class of men. No man was ever turned away who called on him for a charitable purpose.

"We know him but to love him,
We know him but to praise."

Resolved, That the proceedings this meeting be published in the Repu lican papers of the State.

The meeting was a representat one. Nearly all the prominent colo men of the town were present. Y may mark the "little State of Greene" for Wise, Wood, Blair, Gentry, and Sims.

DUDLEY MORTON, President.
R. A. Gibbons, Secretary.

This clipping from an unidentified 1885 newspaper (likely the *Richmond Whig*) records a meeting in Stanardsville of 43 black Republicans from Greene County who were endorsing John S. Wise for governor in that year's election. The article lists the officers of the organizing group as Dudley Morton, A.C. Ramsey, John R.A. Gibbons, and J.W. Coles. It starts by saying "The colored Republicans met here tonight to organize a Wise, Wood, and Blair Club," and concludes "You may mark the 'little State of Greene' for Wise, Wood, Blair, Gentry, and Sims." In the election, Wise was defeated by Fitzhugh Lee, the Democratic candidate. The clipping is pasted into a much older copy book used for math, English, and penmanship lessons. (GCHS, gift of Ethel Dillard.)

105

Dr. E.D. Davis worked in Greene from 1889 to 1934. He was also well known for his civic commitment, serving as clerk of the circuit court. With Kemper Deane, he owned one of the first motor cars in Stanardsville. According to Deane's son Dookie, however, Dr. Davis never drove very well and preferred to visit patients on horseback. (GCHS, gift of Ackline Deane.)

Nathaniel Bezaleel Early, who was born on July 30, 1866, and died on August 15, 1947, served in the Virginia State Legislature first as a representative and then as a senator from 1897 to 1933. He was a major force in ensuring the building of US Route 29 to improve access to and from Greene County. The bridge at Route 29 over the Rapidan River, which separates Greene and Madison Counties, was named for Senator Early. (Richard N. Early.)

Despite the best efforts of the "revenuers," making moonshine was still a profitable enterprise in the 1950s. In October 1956, Sheriff Wilbur "Hooks" Deane is pictured at far left as other officers examine some of dozens of quart canning jars loaded in this vehicle. About 125 gallons of illicit liquor were confiscated during this bust. (Ellen Morris Deane.)

Judge John Joseph Morris, adopted son of Austin and Clementine Morris of Greene, was born in 1907 in Philadelphia but made deep roots in Greene. He died in November 1957. Besides his judicial appointment, other offices he held included mayor of Stanardsville, serving as a Mason, and being a trustee of Blue Ridge School. (Margaret Anne Morris Curran, daughter of John Morris and Genevieve Eddins Morris.)

This photograph was taken on Memorial Day in 1964. Pictured here are, from left to right, T.B.P. Davis, Marguerite Sims Birkhead, Lucy Duff, James Snow, and E.D. Jarman. Davis was one of the speakers. Birkhead and Duff, representing the Spotswood Trail Garden Club, laid wreaths on the two Court Square war memorials. (Julie Dickey.)

In 1967, the Spotswood Trail Garden Club was working on a landscaping project to beautify the area around the courthouse, planting boxwoods and dogwood trees, and took this photograph. Court Square looks very different today. The two-story clerk's office at right was destroyed in the fire 12 years later. In the jail left of the courthouse, which now houses the GCHS museum, a door has replaced the ground-floor window. (Spotswood Trail Garden Club.)

This November 1955 photograph is of Dorothy Banks Morton and her husband, James. Dorothy was born on April 19, 1919, and died on July 14, 2011. She was an active and highly respected member of the community, keenly aware of civic responsibility. In April 1964, she and James were parties to the suit brought against the Greene County School Board to require desegregation in the school system. (Cynthia Carpenter.)

George Wallace may be the only presidential candidate ever to have made a campaign stop in Stanardsville. He came to town on Wednesday, October 30, 1968, while running as the American Independent Party candidate. In Virginia, he lost the race to Republican candidate Richard Nixon. (GCHS, gift of Alec A. Pandaleon III.)

WALLACE

FOR PRESIDENT

GEORGE C. WALLACE

MEETING

GREENE COUNTY COURT HOUSE
Wednesday, Oct. 30th - 7:30 P.M.
STANARDSVILLE, VA.

This horrendous conflagration seared its way into the memories of all who were in Stanardsville on October 24, 1979. The remains of the backhoe that caused the gas leak leading to this destruction are in the foreground, and a wall of fire sweeps from the shell of the county clerk's office (pictured on page 108) towards the courthouse. Efforts by construction workers to shut off the gas supply failed, and although the contents of the clerk's vault were saved by heroic efforts of firefighters and others, irreplaceable records, such as those of the school board, went up in smoke. While rebuilding was underway, administrators and elected county officials used temporary offices, some of which were located on the second floor of the 1838 jail. (Julie Dickey.)

Ten

FAMILIES AND FRIENDS

Morris, Powell, Williams, Jones—these family names are to be expected of people living in the Welsh valleys, and they are just as much a part of Greene County. Ancestors of many families here left Wales—and the rest of the British Isles—in order to find new beginnings in America. When asked if they are connected with another person whose family has long roots here, people from the older families might reply in one of three ways: that the person is kin, close kin, or, with emphasis, "no kin of mine."

Another unique family name has roots in Greene County—the Shiffletts, whether the last name is spelled with one or two Fs, Ls, or Ts. The origins of the name are not clear. Some say they are descendants of escaped Hessian soldiers who were held prisoner in Charlottesville; however, there are pre–Revolutionary War marriage records that contain the Shifflett name. Whatever the origin, if one encounters a Shifflett anywhere in the world, there is a good chance that the person's origins are in Greene. Later generations have gone far afield. Eugene Powell's genealogy database of more than 115,000 names of descendants of Greene County is used to help answer the questions that come to the historical society from all over the country from those investigating their roots.

This final chapter includes two of the many people who made immense contributions to the well-being of the people of Greene County throughout their own lifetimes. One is Nelie Wampler, and the other is Senannie Beaty. Both of these women gave from their hearts to the community and are recognized here with pride.

This c. 1885 image may be Thomas Monroe Shelton and Ella Maupin Shelton's wedding portrait, made in Washington, DC, where Ella was living with her parents. The Shelton family still farms along South River; they own many acres there and once farmed land in the mountains now included in Shenandoah National Park. (GCHS, gift of Marian Durrer.)

This undated photograph of the Long family includes, from left to right, (first row) Perrentus Jackson Long, Azariah Samuel Long, Samuel George Long, Frances Jane Shifflett Long, and Jeremiah Andrew Long; (second row) Mamie Bryant, Alvin Southard (possibly), Isabel Catherine Long, Jeremiah Bryant, Ida Frances Long Bryant, William Henry Brill, Mildred Anne Long Brill, and Edith Long (possibly). (Dorothy R. Bundy.)

This picture shows the Parrott house, which has panoramic views along the South River valley to the Blue Ridge Mountains beyond. It was built around 1895 by John William and Arvonia Lee McMullan Parrott. John and Arvonia's children are pictured here with their parents; they are, from left to right, William Thomas, John Neal, Bertha Ennes (in her mother's arms), Annie Nettie, and Edna Lee. (Bobby Rhodes.)

This photograph taken around 1915 shows James (Jim) Frank Knight and Maggie Lawson, who were married in 1913 when he was 19 and she was almost 20. They had five children. Maggie died when she was 70; Jim outlived her by more than 20 years. (Gerri Gilbert.)

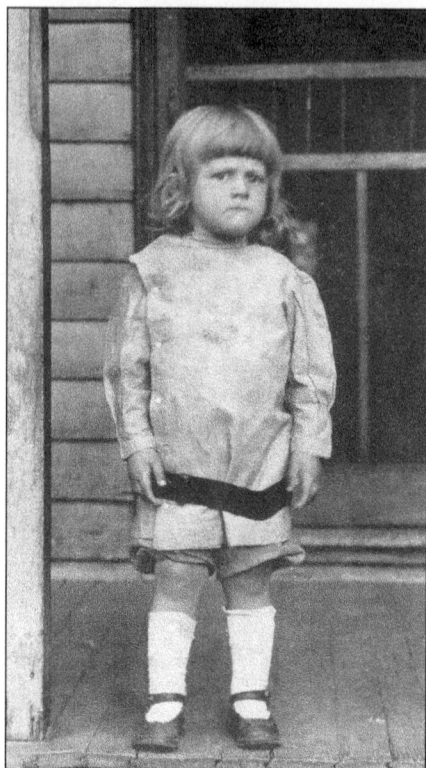

This child may look as if he would give any teacher trouble, but William "Dump" Shelton (1846–1922) became a teacher himself, according to the 1880 census. He joined Company C of the 4th Virginia Cavalry when he was 17 and was wounded in 1865. (GCHS, gift of Marian Durrer.)

This is a late-1890s albumen print portrait of Judson Alfred Fleet Runkle (seated) and George Robert Frazier Runkle. They were the eighth and ninth children of Milt and Berta Beadles Runkle, who married in November 1865. George died in 1903, a few years after this picture was taken, at age 20. (Franklin A. Robinson Jr.)

Harriet (Hattie) Eliza C. Sims Cole was born in 1853; the date she died is not known. A young woman when this undated daguerreotype was made, she was wearing some beautiful jewelry. She married Maurice Newman Cole when she was 21, and by the time she was 47, she had given birth to 11 children. (GCHS.)

Adaline (Addie) Cole was born in Greene County around 1874; she did not marry George M. Stone until 1904, when she was about 30 years old. By the time of the 1910 census, the Stone family was living in Birmingham, Alabama, where George ran a pipe shop. Hattie Cole (shown in the previous photograph) was Addie's aunt by marriage. (GCHS, gift of Marian Durrer.)

Nelie Wampler's name comes up frequently in the history of Greene. Born in Weyers Cave, Virginia, in 1877, she wanted to be a missionary in India but instead came to Greene County in 1909 and stayed to serve the people for 58 years. She is pictured above, seventh from right, with one of the many classes of girls she taught at the Church of the Brethren Industrial School. The photograph below, which is also undated, shows her with produce that is undoubtedly going to good use. Miss Nelie was not overweight; nevertheless, she fasted one day a week and gave the money that would otherwise have bought her food to charity. She died on February 17, 1970, after a lifetime of service. (Above, Olen Morris; below, Ellen Morris Deane.)

Senannie Beaty lived in the beautiful house called Aspengrove (above) in Ruckersville; it was the original home of the Rucker family. The house, which burned in the 1970s, was featured in J.W. Wayland's 1937 book *Historic Homes of Northern Virginia and the Eastern Panhandle of West Virginia.* Beaty, who died on her 95th birthday in 1987, was a well-loved personage. One of her many public spirited acts was embroidering dozens of names on a World War I Red Cross fundraiser signature quilt that is now in the collection of the GCHS. She is shown in the undated image at right at the door of Aspengrove with Thomas Edward Johnson, who was the local newspaper editor in the 1960s and compiled a history of Greene County. (Above, GCHS; right, Julie Dickey.)

This picture of sisters Hazel (left) and Gladys Lamb, daughters of James "Willis" Lamb, was taken in 1927 when they were 14 and 16, respectively. The Lamb family farm was on Middle River. The original photograph has been cut to fit an oval frame. Hazel became the wife of Henry Lamb, the musician and farmer pictured on page 98. (Chelsi Smith.)

This 1920 photograph was taken at the McMullen home place. In the very front is Iris Love McMullen Cartier. Behind her are, from left to right, (second row) Jessie Royal McMullen Walter, Roland Randolph McMullen, Violet Imogene McMullen Crawford, Jubal Early McMullen, Jewell Audrey McMullen Teel, and Neal Hartwell McMullen; (third row) Dulaney Kendall McMullen, Virginia Christian McMullen Grant, John Neal McMullen, Sarah Cornelia McMullen, Nellie Rowe McMullen, Newcombe Pemberton McMullen, and Sarah Antoinette McMullen. (Emily McMullen Williams.)

This photograph of the Dean family was taken in 1924 on the mountain close to the Dean cemetery. From left to right are Beulah, Maggie Rogers Dean (holding baby Clara), Jessie, and Ruby. The treadle sewing machine that Maggie had owned since before her marriage, on which she undoubtedly made many of the family's clothes, is in the GCHS collection and was a gift from Clara. (Clara Dean Herring.)

Benjamin S. Morton was born in Ruckersville as the Civil War was ending; he lived his entire life in Greene County. His wife, Estelle, is listed in the 1940 census as married, but his name does not appear. Morton is shown here with his daughter Amanda in a studio portrait. The original Art Deco frame helps date the photograph to the 1930s. (Cynthia Carpenter.)

119

These undated photographs tell a romantic story. The young Willie Blanche Dulaney Gilbert is pictured at left by herself and below, many years later, with her husband Benjamin Weston Gilbert. Willie, who was from the well-to-do Dulaney family, fell in love with B.W., and he with her. In March 1909, they eloped from Mount Paran Church, driving by horse and buggy to Burnley Station, where they went by train to Washington, DC, and got married; Willie asked her sisters to tell her parents. The couple was married for 44 years and had 13 children. (Both, Gerri Gilbert.)

This studio portrait was taken in the mid-1950s; the painted backdrop of Washington landmarks offers a clue as to the location of the studio. Hattie Taylor Kelley is holding her niece Edith Kenney (left) and her daughter Sylvia Kelley. Originally from Greene County, Hattie Kelley moved to Washington, DC, when she married. (Elizabeth Diane Kenney.)

Although logging was discontinued in the area that became Shenandoah National Park, Eugene L. Eppard's lumber mill on Parker Mountain Road, where this undated photograph was taken, was one of a number that continued to operate in the county. Eppard's shoulders are flecked with sawdust from the mill. (Harold Eppard, son of Eugene.)

Evangeline (Van) Cleage's is one of the few families with Native American ancestry that can be identified in present-day Greene County. Her grandparents, Teeny and Hamilton (Ham) Edward Height, lived at the family farm on Height Road in Ruckersville. Teeny had mostly Native American ancestry. Van, who was a fashion designer, is pictured modeling in Washington in 1951. (Evangeline Cleage.)

In the late 1950s the Taylor siblings were photographed with their mother, Hattie Jane, at the Taylor home, which was on the south side of State Route 33 opposite where the sheriff's office is located today. From left to right are: (first row) Ganaway Roosevelt Taylor and Edward Henry Taylor; (second row) Elisabeth Taylor, Hattie Jane Taylor, Mildred Ann Taylor, and Mary Catherine Taylor. (Estelle Joyner, daughter of Ganaway.)

Bessie May Keyseear was born in Ruckersville in 1909. In 1926, she married Walton Wood; they had their only child, Mary Barbara, the following year. This photograph, taken in an unknown location, is of Bessie and Mary Barbara. Bessie died in 2004, but her stories live on in the memoir that was published by the historical society in the *Greene County Magazine* later that year. (Cynthia Robertson Clatterbuck.)

This is an undated portrait of Gertrude (Trity) Sims and her husband "Fridy" Carter. Trity was born in 1895 in Ruckersville. With a scarcity of jobs in the area, she, like other Sims relatives, eventually moved to West Virginia, where she met and married Fridy. They had no children. (Betty Sims Brown, Trity's great-niece.)

Many family reunions take place in the summertime. The Powell family has been putting on such a gathering since 1927, when it was first organized by Roberta May Powell, Wyatt B. Haney, E.P. Powell, Henrietta Powell Haney, Estelle Kennedy Powell, Haseltine Powell Haney, and Pinkus D. Powell. The first Powell reunions were held at the old Beazley home place on Celt Road, but

now they are usually held at the picnic grounds in Shenandoah National Park near the properties that the families once owned. This photograph was taken at the 1948 reunion and includes at least 120 people. (Joann Powell.)

This splendid house, named Westover, was the home of Sen. Nathaniel B. Early, his wife, Sudie Brent Brown, and their family. The photograph above was taken in 1902; the image below is from 1905. The house still stands, facing spectacular views of the Blue Ridge Mountains, although it is now painted white, and the fine cupola and other decorative woodwork are gone. The photograph below not only shows some prize shorthorn cattle but also some of the detail in the intricate woodwork. Senator Early is in the background, and his son Richard N. Early is in the foreground. (Both, Richard N. Early, grandson of Senator Early.)

Many of the homes and churches in these pages were built by James E. Harlow, also known as "Limpin' Jim." These include the Page house in Stanardsville, Grace Episcopal Church and Westover United Methodist Church, and Senator Early's house, Westover. Harlow was an architect, as well as a carpenter and an innovative builder. He loved the decorative elements of Victorian architecture, as was evident in the houses he constructed. Harlow was also celebrated as something of a poet, with many of his writings appearing in the *Greene County Record*. In this photograph, he stands at the front of the porch of his home in Quinque with his wife, Alice, at his side; the other people are unidentified. The photograph is believed to have been taken shortly before Harlow's death in 1928. (GCHS, gift of Lawrence Perry.)

Visit us at
arcadiapublishing.com

www.ingramcontent.com/pod-product-compliance
Lightning Source LLC
Chambersburg PA
CBHW050628110426
42813CB00007B/1750